RIDDLES ANCIENT AND MODERN

RIDDLES
ANCIENT AND MODERN

Mark Bryant

HUTCHINSON
London Melbourne Sydney Auckland Johannesburg

Hutchinson & Co. (Publishers) Ltd

An imprint of the Hutchinson Publishing Group

17–21 Conway Street, London W1P 6JD

Hutchinson Group (Australia) Pty Ltd
30–32 Cremorne Street, Richmond South, Victoria 3121
PO Box 151, Broadway, New South Wales 2007

Hutchinson Group (NZ) Ltd
32–34 View Road, PO Box 40-086, Glenfield, Auckland 10

Hutchinson Group (SA) (Pty) Ltd
PO Box 337, Bergvlei 2012, South Africa

First published 1983

Set in Bembo by Rowland Phototypesetting Ltd,
Bury St Edmunds, Suffolk

Printed in Great Britain by The Anchor Press Ltd,
and bound by Wm Brendon & Son Ltd,
both of Tiptree, Essex

British Library Cataloguing in Publication Data
Riddles ancient and modern.
  1. Riddles
  I. Bryant, Mark
  793.73'5   PN371.5

ISBN 0 09 151301 4

FOR MY PARENTS

Some people have an unconquerable love of riddles. They may have the chance of listening to plain sense, or to such wisdom as explains life; but no, they must go and work their brains over a riddle, just because they do not understand what it means.

Isak Dinesen, 'The Deluge at Nornderney', *Seven Gothic Tales* (1934)

Et quid amabo nisi quod aenigma est?

Giorgio de Chirico from *Self-Portrait* (1908)

Would'st thou divert thyself from melancholy?
Would'st thou be pleasant, yet be far from folly?
Would'st thou read *riddles* and their explanation?
Or else be drowned in contemplation?
. . . O then come hither
And lay this book, thy head and heart together.

John Bunyan, 'The Author's Apology for His Book' from *The Pilgrim's Progress* (1678)

Contents

Preface

The history of riddling is a rich and varied one and stretches back far into the antiquity of our culture. Indeed, man's observations of analogies in nature led him to invent oral riddles long before he could shape letters and communicate them to others, many of the earliest literary enigmas being reworkings of far older spoken forms. However, the attraction of the riddle in all its many guises – literary, oral and pictorial – has apparently flagged in recent years, most of the surviving relics being allotted a lowly position amongst the comic books and video machines of playroom and amusement arcade. Occasional flames of interest still flicker from time to time, but somehow the spark that was able to set the Middle Ages and the Renaissance ablaze in a riot of enigmatic jollification has come to rest on damp kindling in recent years.

In this book, in what must of necessity be a highly selective and personal choice from the chronicles of the art, I have skimmed fairly rapidly through the history of the riddle, giving a brief overview of the development of the form from its ancient beginnings to the present day, and have added what is, hopefully, a representative sample of what the field has to offer. Obviously there will be many sources I have been unable to consult and though I have tried to be as accurate as possible no pretensions to scholarship are made; I merely commend what follows to the reader as a cursory glimpse of a currently sadly neglected form of entertainment in the hope that some fun, and perhaps even a little further interest, may result.

Regrettably, owing to reasons of economy, it has not been possible to include any illustrations or an intended chapter on pictorial riddles as originally planned. However, I am indebted to the kindness of Danny Nissim, Belinda Thompson, Dione Johnson and Laurence Guernet for much-needed renderings of hitherto untranslated material. Thanks too to Daphne Wright and her team for helping to piece it all together; to Ib Bellew whose crazy idea got the whole thing started; and to my family and friends who always wondered where I was. It only remains for me to wish the reader – as the renowned English emblematist Francis Quarles does in the Preface to his own book *Emblemes* – '. . . as much pleasure in the reading, as I had in the writing'. And I hope you laugh once, at least.

Mark Bryant
London, 1983

Introduction

It may come as some surprise to those who have only encountered riddles in the guise of jokes wrapped round party hats in Christmas crackers, or who have been on the receiving end of witticisms from precocious infants such as 'Why did the chicken cross the road?', that this skittish footnote to the austere chronicles of our folk-culture heritage has itself an ancient and learned history. All those saloon-bar teases over a glass of beer, or stammered opening gambits at not-so-informal cocktail parties are examples of verbal sleights-of-hand whose ancestry can be traced back to classical Greece and beyond.

Did you know that Swift, Schiller, Edgar Allan Poe and Jane Austen all wrote riddles? Or that enigmas were known and discussed by Aristotle and Homer centuries before Freud analysed their relation to jokes and the unconscious? Riddles appear in the Bible, the Koran, and ancient Sanskrit and Norse manuscripts. Writers from St Aldhelm and Cervantes to Goethe, Galileo and Shakespeare either composed riddles themselves or drew on sources from elsewhere to embroider their works. And closer to our own time Puccini, Tolkien and Lewis Carroll have all made use of enigmas in their world-renowned compositions.

One of the earliest known riddles is inscribed on an ancient tablet believed to date from Babylonian times, and reads as follows:

Who becomes pregnant without conceiving?
Who becomes fat without eating?

to which the answer is 'clouds'; whilst the oldest Greek riddle is that propounded in the search for Glaukos, son of Minos, King of Crete and custodian of the infamous Minotaur. As a child, it is said, the unfortunate Glaukos was chasing a mouse through the palatial store-rooms when he tripped and fell into an enormous vat of honey and expired. Minos, failing to find the boy anywhere, consulted his soothsayers, who in true oracular form came up with the following:

> In the fields grazeth a calf whose body changeth hue thrice in the space of each day. It is first white, then red, and at the last black. He who can unravel the meaning of this riddle will restore thy child to thee alive.

The answer, a mulberry, was supplied by one Polyidos, who subsequently discovered Glaukos in the vat and miraculously restored him to life. Minos forced Polyidos to tell Glaukos the secret of his resurrection. The seer eventually did so, but was so incensed at his treatment that as he sailed off he spat into the boy's mouth, stopping his memory of the secret for ever.

But the history of the riddle goes back even beyond these records to the very infancy of the human race, arising spontaneously along with folk-songs and proverbs in the dawn of man's primitive existence on this planet.

Anatomy of the Riddle

So just what exactly is a riddle? On closer inspection this proves to be a thornier subject than it first appears, as many authorities hold differing opinions as to what should and what should not be included under this rubric. Indeed, one of the most influential thinkers of modern times, Ludwig Wittgenstein (1889–1951), had very definite views on riddling as he shows in *Tractatus Logico-Philosophicus* (1921):

> The *riddle* does not exist.
> If a question can be framed at all, it is also possible to answer it.

– a view shared by Edgar Allan Poe (1809–49) in a short story called 'The Gold Bug':

> It may well be doubted whether human ingenuity can construct an enigma of the kind which human ingenuity may not, by proper application, resolve.

– though it is curious that the great philosopher should assume that riddles are unanswerable by definition and hence do not exist.

However, academic wrangles apart, I shall outline here a

general working description of what I think most people would agree to be the essential bones of the topic, which, though of necessity somewhat skeletal, should be adequate for the purposes of this brief introduction.

To clear the ground it is of course first necessary to distinguish our word from that meaning 'a coarse-meshed sieve' or 'a board or metal plate set with pins used in straightening wire' which derives from the Old English *hriddel*, 'to sift'. According to the *Oxford English Dictionary* the word 'riddle' in the sense of this book has its origins in the Old English *raedels* meaning 'advice' or 'opinion', and the definition given there is the following rather general description:

> A question or statement intentionally worded in a dark or puzzling manner, and propounded in order that it may be guessed or answered, especially as a form of pastime; an enigma, a dark saying.

If, from this kind of 'dark saying', we follow the cross-reference to 'enigma', we find that this comes from the Greek verb meaning 'to speak allusively (or obscurely)' and the noun 'a fable'. But what distinguishes a riddle from other kinds of 'dark sayings', such as parables, proverbs, fables, or simple grammatical and arithmetical puzzles, is its use of metaphor. Broadly speaking, a 'true' riddle is one that compares two otherwise unrelated things in a metaphorical manner and is usually verbal, either written or spoken. Obviously the descriptions must be as accurate as possible or the point will be lost, but they are deliberately phrased in such a way as to baffle and puzzle the reader or listener. A riddle may take the form of a statement or a question, sometimes prefixed by an interrogative formula such as 'Riddle me, riddle me ree' (itself a corruption of 'Riddle me a riddle, riddle my riddle').

The oral riddle is a simple unembellished puzzle which has been passed down by word of mouth and whose solution is usually a familiar object, natural phenomenon, etc. These riddles can be found in all societies at all times in history, but are particularly prevalent in those areas which are technologically under-developed. A very simple example of such a riddle is the children's rhyme of Humpty Dumpty, who appears to be a man but is in fact nothing more than an egg.

Almost by definition, most *recorded* oral riddles have become slightly more literary in the very act of writing them down, but the true literary riddle is one which has been deliberately crafted around the written form. Thus they may have complicated metres and/or rhyming schemes and may be embroidered with delicate metaphors. Their solutions are also generally far more wide-ranging, and often include some of a more abstract nature. Here is an example, on a rainbow, by one of the acknowledged masters of the art, Friedrich von Schiller (1759–1805):

A bridge of pearls its form uprears
   High o'er a grey and misty sea;
E'en in a moment it appears,
   And rises upwards giddily.

Beneath its arch can find a road
   The loftiest vessel's mast most high,
Itself hath never borne a load,
   And seems, when thou draw'st near, to fly.

It comes first with the stream, and goes
   Soon as the wat'ry flood is dried.
Where may be found this bridge, disclose,
   And who its beauteous form supplied!

Apart from the 'true' riddles there are also a number of related forms of puzzle which would normally be called 'riddles' and which, for that reason, I have included in this book.

The *conundrum* is a riddle whose solution is based on the punning use of words in the question. Thus the conundrum 'What is black and white and red all over?', which seems to signify a strange multi-coloured beast, is answered by the solution 'a newspaper' – the puns working on 'red' and 'all over'. Conundrums are apparently quite a recent addition to the riddler's armoury and today appeal particularly to children.

A *charade* is a variety which appears to have had its origins in the Languedoc region of France (the word itself being French). Again a relatively recent development in riddling history it is essentially a literary exercise playing on letters or syllables, and as such has been called the *Silbenrätsel* (syllable riddle) in German. A well-known charade by the eighteenth-century Whig statesman Charles James Fox runs as follows:

My *first* is expressive of no disrespect,
   But I never call you by it when you are by;

If my *second* you still are resolved to reject,
As dead as my *whole*, I shall presently lie.

The answer is 'herring' (her-ring). Charades can also be acted out and in this form are still a very popular kind of parlour game.

Logogriphs, also known as *Worträtsel* or *calembours*, are riddles based on single words in which letters are removed to make new words. They are thus concerned with the form of the word and its components rather than its meaning. A French version drawn from the eighteenth-century literary magazine *Mercure de France* will serve to illustrate this: *'Je brille avec six pieds, avec cinq je te couvre.'* This signifies the word *'étoile'* (star) which, by losing a letter, becomes *'toile'* (tablecloth). The logical development of this form, involving the transposition of the letters themselves, is the anagram.

Even more concerned with the position of words and letters is the *literary rebus*. A very simple rebus using letters on their own would be 'IOU' (for 'I owe you'), or the caption of Duchamp and Picabia's notorious bearded version of the Mona Lisa (1919), 'LHOOQ' *(Elle a chaud au cul)*. A simple but even cleverer French rebus consists of just two letters, G and a, to be read *J'ai grand appetit (G grand, a petit)*. Many rebuses also involve the positioning of words and letters, such as the following representation of 'I understand he undertook to overthrow this undertaking':

stand	took	to	taking
I	he	throw	this

or the French:

pir	vent	venir
un	vient	d'un

which is to be read *Un soupir vient souvent d'un souvenir*.

'Catch' riddles are, strictly speaking, hardly riddles at all in any sense of the word but are more like jokes, whose humour derives from the fact that they seem to imply by their riddle-like form that a witty solution is in order, when in fact the answer really is the obvious one. 'Why did the chicken cross the road? To get to the other side' is a widely used example of this kind. Related to these are other kinds of trick riddle either in the form of arithmetical puzzles such as:

A priest, and a friar, and a silly auld man,
Gaed [went] to a pear tree, where three pears hang.
Lika [each] ane took a pear – how many hang there?

– the answer being 'two', as the three men are the same person – or those of the 'hidden name' variety:

There was a king met a king
    In a straight lane;
Says the king to the king
    Where have you been?
I've been in the wood,
    Hunting the doe:
Pray lend me your dog,
    That I may do so.
Call him, call him!
    What must I call him?
Call him as you and I,
    We've done both.

The dog's name is 'Been'.

There are also *pictorial riddles*, where allegorical statements are made by images, leading to a moral that is revealed by the 'solution' of the picture. In other varieties a name or saying may be discovered by punning use of the words used to describe the objects. Pictorial puzzles of this kind obviously owe much to the hieroglyphics of the ancient Egyptians and other picture-based languages and find their modern counterpart in emblems, visual rebuses and, ultimately, via the cryptic paintings of de Chirico and *Pittura metafisica*, in certain aspects of the work of the Surrealist Movement.

Riddles occur too in the world of music. Tchaikovsky is on record as having described his Sixth Symphony ('Pathétique') as being something of a riddle, based on a programme which 'is of a kind which remains an enigma to all – let them guess it who can'. Solutions such as Life, Love, Disillusionment and Death have been suggested but the programme remains a mystery. In a similar vein are the *Enigma Variations* of Edward Elgar. Composed in 1899, they are a deliberate attempt to capture in music the personalities of certain of Elgar's friends. Although he gave clues to the solutions of the musical riddles in the form of their subjects' initials, and later identified the personalities themselves, a further enigma remains, as the overall theme running through the whole piece is supposed to conceal a popular melody. Various suggestions have been made, from 'God Save the King' to 'Auld Lang Syne' (the current favourite of musicologists being 'Rule Britannia'). But the secret of the *Enigma* theme died with its composer.

Moving on to vocal music, one of the characters in Gilbert and Sullivan's *The Yeomen of the Guard* (1888), the prankster Jack Point, is renowned for his riddling and jokes and is most put out when the conversation takes a change of direction after he has put his 'best conundrum' – 'Why is a cook's brain like an overwound clock?' – thereby depriving us of the answer for ever. However, perhaps more accessible to final solution are the riddles contained in Puccini's romantic opera *Turandot*, in which the eponymous heroine, the daughter of a Chinese emperor, consents to marry the first royal suitor who can solve her three riddles – on penalty of death for failure. Prince Calaf, travelling incognito, solves them but is nearly executed when Turandot reneges on her promise. However, all turns out happily in the end and they are eventually married. The riddles, which differ somewhat from those in Gozzi's original (1762) version and those in Schiller's translation, occur in the second act. Here is one on 'hope':

> In the dark night flies a many-hued phantom.
> It soars and spreads its wings
> above the gloomy human crowd.
> The whole world calls to it,
> the whole world implores it.
> At dawn the phantom vanishes
> to be reborn in every heart.
> And every night 't is born anew
> and every day it dies!

The Uses of Riddles and Riddling

Riddles have many uses, but the most widespread throughout their history has been in deciding contests of wit. Such contests have varied from light-hearted entertainments to dramatic battles with a man's fortune or life itself at stake.

In some parts of the world it was once traditionally the custom to grant a condemned man the opportunity of putting a 'neck' riddle to his captors which, if they failed to solve it, would literally save his neck. Naturally the riddles tended to be as esoteric as possible, involving enough specialist and personal knowledge to make them virtually insoluble to any but the propounder. A very famous example is the Ilo riddle: 'On Ilo I walk, on Ilo I stand, Ilo I hold fast in my hand', where Ilo was in fact the riddler's dog, out of whose skin he had made a pair of shoes and a pair of gloves. A still more macabre version of this kind of riddle is the following:

> I sat wi' my love, and I drank wi' my love,
>   And my love she gave me light;
> I'll give any man a pint o' wine,
>   That'll read my riddle right.

(I sat in a chair made from my wife's bones and drank from her skull under a candle made from the fat of her body.)

A natural variant of the 'neck' riddle is that used in a contest for someone's hand in marriage. It was just such a contest that led to the final tragedy of Oedipus. The goddess Hera was angered by the news that the club-footed prince had killed King Laius of Thebes (his father) at the crossroads to the city, and took it upon herself to destroy the good citizens of Boeotia. To this end she sent from Ethiopia the horrendous monster known as the Sphinx, which was the terrible issue of the hundred-headed Typhon and Echidna. Transmogrified from three separate animals, the Sphinx had the face of a woman, the body, feet and tail of a lion, and the wings of a bird, and, as though that was not monster enough to sort out the Boeotians, the canny creature also posed the following riddle to every passer-by:

> What is it that goes on four legs in the morning, two legs at noon and three legs in the evening?

All who failed to solve it were summarily killed. Oedipus, however, guessed the answer to be 'man', who crawls on all fours as a child, walks on two legs as an adult and hobbles on three (the third being a stick) in old age. The Sphinx was so enraged at its defeat that it hurled itself into the nearest abyss. But the winner of the contest was no luckier: the prize for defeating the monster was the hand of Laius's wife and all his worldly goods. Oedipus accepted, still unaware of his true identity, thus fulfilling the prophecy that he would murder his father and marry his mother.

An equally grim contest was that between Thor and the astute underground dwarf Alvis ('all-wise'), who wished to marry Thor's daughter Thrud. Described in the 'Alvissmal' in the *Elder Edda*, this is the earliest known account of a riddle contest for the hand of a lady. Thor puts to the dwarf thirteen questions about the nature of the universe. The god is impressed by Alvis's knowledgeable answers but in the end confesses that the whole test was a ruse to prevent the dwarf's marriage to Thrud, saying:

> Never have I met such a master of lore
>> With such a wealth of wisdom.
> I talked to trick you, and tricked you I have:
>> Dawn has broken, Dwarf,
>> Stiffen now to stone.

(which is apparently what they do if caught in daylight).

However, somewhat more light-hearted competitions are narrated in the riddle ballads of the eighteenth century such as 'Captain Wedderburn's Courtship' and 'A Noble Riddle Wisely Expounded'. And light-hearted is indeed what the riddle-session became in the hands of some exponents, as the delightful frivolity of Straparola's *Facetious Nights (Tredeci Piacevoli Notti)* bears witness. In the introduction to this source-book of drollery the author (whose pseudonym means 'the babbler') explains how Sforza, Duke of Milan, having been ousted from his own court by intrigue, has removed himself to the island of Murano near Venice, and that the book is supposed to be a documentary of the happenings at his palace there during the thirteen nights of Carnival when members of his daughter's circle of friends draw lots to relate stories, sing songs and propound riddles. First published (in a complete edition) in 1557, the book immediately scandalized the local authorities with its earthy enigmas and ribald tales, but surprisingly it was not banned until fifty years later. And even then it was only the allusions to impropriety on the part of various clerical characters in the stories and not the overall licentiousness of the book itself that provoked the Vatican censor's displeasure.

To be fair, though, Straparola was not the only riddler to be tempted into scurrility. Owing to the natural propensity of the riddle form to be used to depict harmless objects in an apparently obscene way, riddles have also been used by many other authors (a surprising number of them from clerical backgrounds) to titillate, shock and scandalize those who hear them. Amongst these must be classified a fair number of the output of the fourteenth-century Bohemian monk Dr Claretus, a good deal from the anonymous author of the *Demaundes Joyous* (the first riddle book ever printed in England) and the vast majority of the works of many Italian enigmatographers of the sixteenth, seventeenth and eighteenth centuries, notably the exceedingly licentious Tommaso Stigliani whose books, along with those of Straparola, were put on the Vatican's index of prohibited titles (1605) to protect public morals. (The full text of Stigliani's *Rime* remains withdrawn from public consumption even to this day.)

Political as well as personal use was made of 'dark sayings' both by soothsayers and their audiences at the oracles of Ancient Greece and Rome. (Needless to say, of course, the prognostications of these sulphur-crazed hags were highly adaptable and capable of a wide range of interpretations.) During the eighteenth century groups of young French lawyers in Picardy used pictorial riddles to lampoon local dignitaries without risk of libel, and it is even said that Lorenzo de' Medici went so far as to employ professional riddlers to distract the populace from his political intrigues.

Another major use of the enigma has been in the performance of religious ceremonies. The telling of riddles on the Jewish Passover Eve is a well-known and long-established tradition, and the long, questioning, 'Who knoweth one?' verse is close to the hearts of all members of the faith from rabbi to bar mitzvah boy. Again we hear of riddles being used almost like a charm in wedding, fertility, harvest and rain-making ceremonies in Africa and elsewhere, Sir James Frazer in *The Golden Bough* (1890–1915) recording examples from an Indonesian ritual to make the rice grow involving the incantation of riddles of every variety. Riddles were also enjoyed at the Roman festival of Saturnalia; the Greeks indulged in the pastime during Agrionia; and it still survives in a lesser form in some modern Christmas celebrations.

Riddles have also been used in teaching everything from religion to grammar. Catechetic and other kinds of 'clever question' involving intimate knowledge of certain scriptures are cases in point. The first section of Pseudo Bede's *Flores*, parts of the somewhat bawdy *Demaundes Joyous* (1511), certain Hindu texts and many of the medieval 'dialogues' all contain examples. Here is an illustration from the fourteenth-century *Dialogue of Salomon and Saturnus:*

> Tell me, who was he that was never born, was then buried in his mother's womb, and after death was baptized?

to which the solution is 'Adam'. And, on the grammatical side, the eleventh-century Arab scholar, story-teller and intelligence chief Al-Hariri includes the following riddle in his twenty-fourth 'assembly':

> And in what place do males put on the veils of women, and the ladies of the alcove go forth with the turbans of men?

which refers to the grammatical ambiguity in Arabic in which the feminine numerals from three to ten are used with masculine nouns and the masculine numerals with feminine nouns. And earlier still, the eighth-century Archbishop of Canterbury, Tatwine, had even composed an enigma on prepositions and the cases they govern in Latin.

Few modern teachers would go to such lengths to thrust learning down the unwilling throats of their pupils, but riddling remains as popular as ever with children. Indeed, the timelessness of the riddle form, and the fact that there are certain kinds of enigma whose humour maintains its freshness all down the ages, seems to suggest that the art of enigmatography is ingrained in our collective unconscious. For as the philosopher Franz Brentano says in the foreword to his book *Neue Räthsel* (1878), '"Astonishment [*Erstaunung*]," said Aristotle, "is and was from the beginning what led men to philosophize; they felt a yearning to the solution of riddles."'

PART ONE

A Brief History of Riddles and Riddling

CHAPTER ONE

Ancient Riddles: Sacred and Profane

Most of the myths of classical antiquity, whether sacred or profane, Greek, Roman, Hebrew, Scandinavian or Asian, are steeped in accounts of riddle contests between men, gods and sundry wise monsters, many of which will already be familiar to the modern reader. Some contests, such as those between Oedipus and the Sphinx, Solomon and Sheba, or Samson and the Philistines, are immediately recognizable, though others, such as the Norse saga of Heidrek and Gestumblindi or the riddle hymn of the Rig-Veda, may be less well known. But all are examples of a riddlemania that had become firmly established as a major art form alongside the traditions of poetry, epitaph- and song-writing long before the new civilizations of mainland Europe had even begun to stir from inarticulate barbarity.

The Classical Riddle

The Greeks in particular were great riddlers. Whether it was a friendly bout of wit after a meal, as described in Athenaeus's *Deipnosophistae* where the loser was condemned to quaff a great mug of wine mixed with brine, or whether in deadly earnest – with rather more sobering penalties – the enigmatic form was a recognized part of classical Greek culture. As in later generations, to be able to give a good account of oneself in this tortuous art was a sign of intellectual prowess and the mark of a wise man.

Though Aesop's *Fables* and some of the pithy pronouncements of Pythagoras of Samos were described as enigmas in their day, the first use of the word with its modern connotation was by the poet Pindar (*c.* 522–442 BC), though there is good reason to believe that the form had existed before. The great pre-Socratic philosopher Heraclitus – now sadly perhaps only generally known as the subject of William Johnson Cory's jingle 'They told me Heraclitus, they told me you were dead,/ They brought me bitter news to hear, and bitter tears to shed.' – was so well known for his cryptic remarks about the nature of the universe that even Cicero and Diogenes Laertius referred to him as 'the Riddler' and 'the Obscure'. Plato refers to the pastime of riddling in *The Republic* and mentions (Book V.479) 'the children's riddle about the eunuch hitting the bat and what he threw at it and what it was sitting on' (this is a variant of Panarces's riddle, viz: a man who was not a man [a eunuch] threw a stone that was not a stone [a pumice stone] at a bird that was not a bird [a bat] sitting on a twig that was not a twig [a reed]). Indeed, the very nature of the riddle itself became a topic for philosophical debate, with Aristotle's Cypriot pupil, Clearchus of Soli, even going so far as to write an entire treatise specifically devoted to the subject (not unnaturally entitled *On Riddles*) in which he distinguished seven different kinds. And Diogenes Laertius, in his *Lives of Eminent Philosophers*, profiles the venerable enigmatographer Cleobulus (*c.*600 BC) who is said to have written over 3,000 lines of songs and riddles. Cleobulus also appears as one of the seven in Plutarch's *Dinner of the Seven Wise Men* as does his equally famous daughter Cleobulina who composed enigmas in hexameters. Another guest at the dinner, Cleodorus, is rounded upon by Aesop for saying of her:

> Perhaps it is not unbecoming for her to amuse herself and to weave these as other girls weave girdles and hair-nets, and to propound them to women, but the idea that men of sense should take them at all seriously is ridiculous.

On the less esoteric side, though perhaps more ridiculous, we hear of Pindar's riddling ode against the letter S; and numerous examples occur in the writings of Antiphanes (including some put in the mouth of the heroine in *Sappho*) and other notable playwrights of the period. There are enigmas in the *Idylls* of Theocritus, Alexis's *Sleep*, Diphilus's *Theseus* and Aristophanes's *Wasps*, as well as umpteen examples in Book 10 of Athenaeus's gallimaufry of classical lore, the *Deipnosophistae*, when the grammarian Aemilianus Maurus decides it is time to turn their discussion away from the pleasures of drink and drinking.

In the surviving fragment of Hesiod's *Melampodie* a riddle contest to the death between the two seers Colchos and Mopsos is described, and in real life the great bard Homer – himself a distinguished enigmatographer – is reputed to have died from chagrin at being unable to solve the following riddle on lice, posed by the fishermen of Ios:

What we caught we threw away; what we didn't catch we kept.

Tales also abound of how Alexander the Great (no doubt well prepared by his tutor Aristotle) picked the wits of the Hindus with riddles, and how Aesop was forever coming to the rescue of King Lycurgus of Babylon in his intellectual battles with the riddling Nectarebo of Egypt.

The well-known riddles of Glaukos and Oedipus can be found throughout Greek literature and many other traditional enigmas of every variety may also be discovered in Book 14 of *The Greek Anthology*, a selection from which appears in Part 2 (see pages 133–4). The following anonymous contribution may serve as a good illustration here:

I am the black child of a white father; a wingless bird, flying even to the clouds of heaven. I give birth to tears of mourning in pupils that meet me, and at once on my birth I am dissolved into air.

The answer is 'smoke' (the pupils are those of the eyes).

Even the Romans, whose comparatively modern culture was based on a regimentation so severe that the reader might be forgiven for doubting their inclination to riddling, are known to have indulged in the art, and riddling continued to flourish during the great age of Latin civilization. The story survives that when Marcus Aurelius asked the Jewish sage Judah the Patriarch how he should go about filling his empty treasury, the patriarch is reported to have gone into his garden and uprooted all the old flowers and planted new ones in their stead. This enacted riddle was taken to mean that the emperor should oust his old councillors and recruit new ones in their place (who would presumably pay for the privilege). A similar story is told of how Tarquin the Great lopped off the heads of the biggest poppies in his garden to signify to Sextus that the chief citizens of the recently conquered Gabii should be executed.

The Roman grammarian Pompeius described the employment of the ice riddle ('My mother brought me forth, then shortly I her daughter brought her forth again') by small boys playing in the streets of classical Rome, and on a more literary note Virgil's third eclogue ('Are these Meliboeus' Sheep?') from the *Pastoral Poems* involves a light-hearted riddling contest between the two shepherds, Menalcas and Damoetas, for the love of a certain Phyllis (see Part 2, page 191).

The Egyptian Greek Athenaeus, though describing events in the Golden Age of Greek literature, was of course himself writing in the time of the Roman Empire (second–third centuries AD) and riddles can also be found in the *Noctes Atticae* of Aulus Gellius, like the following from Book XII.vi:

> I know not if he's minus once or twice,
> Or both of these, who would not give his place
> As I once heard it said, to Jove himself.

The answer to this is 'Terminus' (once *minus* plus twice *minus* is thrice [*ter*] *minus*) and the allusion is to a statue of this god which could not be moved from the temple of Jupiter on the Capitol. The great orator Cicero is also alleged to have penned a few enigmas; Apuleius's lost work *Liber ludicorum et gryphorum* is supposed to have contained a fair number; and riddles also occur in Plutarch's *Dinner of the Seven Sages*. The following triple enigma occurs in Petronius's *Satyricon*:

> 'What part of us am I? I come far, I come wide. Now find me.'
> I can tell you what part of us runs and does not move from its place;
> what grows out of us and grows smaller.

The answers 'foot', 'eye', and 'hair' have been suggested.

Sanskrit and Norse Enigmas

The oldest Sanskrit riddles (*c.*1000 BC) occur in the riddle hymn of Dirghatamas (Hymn 164) in Book I of the Rig-Veda. Of the fifty-two verses all but one are riddles and tend to be on cosmological themes. A good example is the following to which the solutions 'wind' and 'lightning' have been suggested:

> The one who made him does not know him. He escapes from the one who has seen him. Enveloped in his mother's womb, he is subject to annihilation, while he has many descendants.

Again in the 'Vana Parva' of that enormous epic the *Mahabharata* (seven times longer than the *Odyssey* and *Iliad* put together) we find that the riddles form an integral part of the story. Here Yudhisthira and his four royal brothers are dying of thirst in a forest when they come to an enchanted pool. As Yudhisthira arrives he discovers to his horror all the princes lying dead and the pool presided over by a *yaksha* (a servant of the gods normally friendly to man) in the shape of a crane. As he's about to drink the water the *yaksha* threatens to kill him (like all the rest) unless he can first answer its riddles. The questions posed mostly require answers of a moral or religious kind, thus:

Yaksha:	Still, tell me what foeman is worst to subdue?
	And what is the sickness lasts lifetime all through?
	Of men that are upright, say which is the best?
	And of those that are wicked, who passeth the rest?
Yudhisthira:	Anger is man's unconquered foe;
	The ache of greed doth never go;
	Who loveth most of saints is first;
	Of bad men cruel men are worst.

There are nine groups of questions in all, mostly of four lines, and Yudhisthira's reward for answering all correctly is to drink the water and choose one brother's life. He chooses Nakula, a step-brother by another marriage in preference over his own direct kin so that both mothers might rejoice. The *yaksha* is so impressed by this decision that it revives all four of the dead princes.

Apart from the story of Alvis and Thor mentioned earlier, one of the most famous instances of riddling in Norse literature occurs in the tale of King Heidrek in the *Hervarar Saga*. In this we are told how the wise King Heidrek had made a vow to the god Frey that however deeply a man had wronged him he would either be given a fair trial by his seven judges or would be let off scot-free if he could propound a riddle that the king could not answer. Now in his realm dwelt one Gestumblindi who was not on good terms with Heidrek and was in the course of time summoned to be judged according to the custom. Knowing that he would be no match for the king's wit and fearing for his life, Gestumblindi prayed fervently to Odin to help him. His prayers were answered and Odin, dressed as the old man, appeared at Heidrek's hall and posed a number of short riddles like the following:

I saw maidens like dust. Rocks were their beds. They were black and swarthy in the sunshine, but the darker it grew, the fairer they appeared.

– to which the solution is 'embers on the hearth'. Heidrek solved all these without much difficulty, but when Odin asked, 'What did Odin whisper in Balder's ear, before he was placed on the pyre?', the king realized that his opponent could only be Odin himself to know the answer and threw his sword Tyrfing at the god. Odin, however, made good his escape in the form of a falcon but was so piqued by Heidrek's unsporting behaviour that he caused his slaves to murder him that very evening. An attractive variant of this story, set in verse, occurs in the *Gátu Ríma*, or 'Faroese Riddle Ballad' (see Part 2, pages 162–3).

The Judaeo-Christian Tradition

Riddles abound in the Old Testament, and we are constantly reminded in Judaeo-Christian literature that skill in the art of riddling was the mark of a true sage. This astuteness is mentioned in the first chapter of Proverbs which suggests that by following its dictates the reader can acquire wisdom:

> If the wise man listens, he will increase his learning, and the man of understanding will acquire skill to understand proverbs and parables, the sayings of wise men and their riddles.

The One True God himself spoke in riddles and 'dark sayings', though to his chosen few (such as Daniel or Moses) all great knowledge was made plain:

> But my servant Moses is not such a prophet;
>   he alone is faithful of all my household.
>   With him I speak face to face,
>   openly and not in riddles.
> He shall see the very form of the Lord.

> (Numbers 12:7–8)

Many of the Proverbs are also believed to have been originally current as riddles before being written down. For example, Proverbs 17:12 could be redrafted as the enigma: 'What is worse than meeting a bear? Meeting a fool in his folly.' Proverbs 30 is actually a true riddle about the four mysterious things, the four little wise things and the four stately things, the second group of which I quote here (for the entire riddle see Part 2, page 112):

> Four things there are which are smallest on earth
>> yet wise beyond the wisest:
>> ants, a people with no strength
>> yet they prepare their store of food in the summer;
>> rock-badgers, a feeble folk,
>> yet they make their home among the rocks;
>> locusts, which have no king,
>> yet they sally forth in detachments;
>> the lizard, which can be grasped in the hand,
>> yet is found in the palaces of kings.

The prophet Daniel, dragged off to Babylon in captivity with the rest of the Israelites when they were conquered by the Chaldeans, could not only hold his own with the odd lion but also had an enviable reputation as a solver of puzzles, and was much sought out by the noble insomniacs and perplexed dignitaries of the day:

> This same Daniel . . . is known to have a notable spirit, with knowledge and understanding, and the gift of interpreting dreams, explaining riddles and unbinding spells.
>
> (Daniel 5:12)

To this end, it was Daniel who was summoned to untangle the meaning of the celestial graffiti that became manifest at the feast of King Belshazzar: *Mene, mene, tekel, upharsin.* Literally 'mina, mina, shekel, half-mina' (units of currency), Daniel took this to mean that Belshazzar had been 'numbered, numbered, weighed and found wanting', which in concrete terms signified that his time was up and that his kingdom would be split up and given to the Medes and Persians, which is indeed what happened.

The riddle proposed by the Hebrew judge Samson to a group of Philistines gathered at his wedding reception is justly acclaimed, and apart from its appearance in Holy Writ has been widely disseminated throughout the Western world in recent years on the green-and-gold tins of Tate & Lyle's Golden Syrup:

> Out of the eater came forth something to eat
> Out of the strong came forth something sweet.
>
> (Judges 14:14)

Samson in his wisdom gave the fellows seven days to solve the riddle and stipulated a forfeit of 'thirty fine linen wrappers and thirty gala dresses' for the loser. Admittedly it was a somewhat unfair contest as the solution relied on special knowledge – the fact that Samson had seen in the desert a lion's carcass in which bees had made a hive – but with the help of his new bride the Philistines returned to the court with the answer, itself phrased in the form of a riddle: 'What is sweeter than honey? What is stronger than a lion?' (to which some commentators have appended the solution 'love'). Samson, somewhat peeved at this subterfuge, riddled out his anger in the following words: 'If you had not ploughed with my heifer, you would not have found out my riddle,' and paid his debt by murdering thirty Philistines and giving *their* clothes to the winners.

But perhaps the greatest of all the biblical enigmatographers, and certainly one of the wisest men in the Hebrew tradition, was King Solomon of Jerusalem, architect of the great temple, author of the bestselling Song of Songs and Ecclesiastes, and constantly quoted worthy in all matters of judgement and law. In the first Book of Kings the scribe tells us how Bilqis, Queen of Sheba, travelled many miles to Solomon's court with the express purpose of testing out his prodigious wisdom, posing many 'hard questions' to the great man in cryptic form. Though these are not reported in the Bible itself, some held to be the genuine article can be found in the 2nd Targum to the Book of Esther and elsewhere in rabbinical literature – the best of them being:

Without movement while living, it moves when its head is cut off.

and

Produced from the ground, man produces it, while its food is the fruit of the ground.

The solution to the former is 'tree', which when its head (branches) is cut off can be made into a ship, and to the latter is 'wick'. (See also Part 2, page 156.) Solomon's riddling talent appears again in the chronicles of the great Jewish historian Josephus (*Antiquities of the Jews*, Chapter 8: 3) where we learn of Solomon and Hiram of Tyre sparring at riddles by post:

. . . the king of Tyre sent sophisms and enigmatical sayings to Solomon and desired he would solve them, and free them from the ambiguity that was in them.

In this case the forfeit was cash and Hiram soon began to lose heavily until he unearthed in the backstreets of his kingdom a crack riddle-solver called Abdemon who quickly won back the money from Solomon, and more besides.

Apart from those of the Old Testament, a number of riddles can also be found in the Talmud, many of which play on letters of the Hebrew alphabet, but some, like 'What animal has one voice living and seven voices dead?' (answer: 'ibis', from whose carcass many instruments can be made), are genuine riddles.

There is even a poetical riddle, the solution to which has never clearly been established:

High from heav'n her eye looks down,
Constant strife excites her frown;
Winged beings shun her sight,
She puts the youth to instant flight.
The aged too her looks do scout;
Oh! oh! the fugitive cries out.
And by her snares whoe'er is lured
Can never of his sin been cured.

Another as yet unsolved riddle occurs in the Revelation of St John (the only riddle in the Christian New Testament):

He that hath understanding let him count the number of the beast; for it is the number of a man, and his number is six hundred and sixty and six.

A number of interpretations have been put forward over the centuries but none seems to be wholly satisfactory, a fact that might lead one to conclude, as did G. K. Chesterton generally, that 'The riddles of God are more satisfying than the solutions of man.'

CHAPTER TWO
Modern Beginnings

The roots of modern literary riddling in the Western world can be traced back to the incursions of the Saxons and Norsemen into England in the centuries following the departure of the Romans in AD 406. With them the Teutonic hordes brought to these windy isles a tradition of wandering minstrel poets that related sagas of heroes from former times, and a homespun craze for enigmatic and metaphorical descriptions of all kinds. The new race of Anglo-Saxons quickly developed their own cryptic sayings from these earlier Germanic 'kennings' and developed an enigmatic art form that was soon to hold its own amongst the other varieties of literature of the period. But more than anything it was the growth of classical erudition, particularly as encouraged by King Alfred – who imported scholars like Hadrian from the ancient cultures of the Mediterranean with their already-established heritage of enigmatography – that gave rise to the important Anglo-Latin school of riddle-masters who in their turn paved the way for all riddling, whether in Latin or the vernacular, to follow. Starting with the 'century' (100) of enigmas finely crafted by an anonymous learned scribe some time around the fifth century AD, renewed interest in the art of riddling, both pagan and religious, spread across the mainland of Europe and into the Far East where it mingled with indigenous traditions of cryptic utterance formed from time immemorial.

Symphosius and the Anglo-Latin School

The father of modern literary riddling and inspiration for all subsequent riddle-masters up to the Renaissance is himself surrounded in clouds of enigma. He is acknowledged as 'Symphosius' by his great successor Aldhelm, but whether this was his real name, a pseudonym for one of the minor Latin poets, Firmianius Symphosius Caelius or Lactantius (under whose names his work was widely disseminated), or whether the name merely describes what the riddles were used for – i.e. post-prandial intellectual discourse (cf. Plato's *Symposium*) – is a matter for academic dispute. What is certain is that one hundred hexameter triplets in good, if prosaic, Latin on subjects varying from everyday items (and lots of bugs, lice and worms) to celestial phenomena were carefully copied out and grouped under the title *Symphosii Aenigmata*. Generally believed to have been composed somewhere around the fifth century AD, and decidedly pagan in character, they were enormously popular in Anglo-Saxon England and have remained so ever since. Indeed, such has been Symphosius's influence that he has come to be regarded as doing for the riddle what Martial did for the epigram, being held up as a model and ideal to be strived towards by all the great riddlers that followed. The riddles were originally devised for recitation at the ancient feast of Saturnalia, a traditional forum for enigmas and jests, and the carnival atmosphere is reflected in the verse.

The collection, which contains many literary inventions as well as versifications of folk themes, also includes a version of Homer's lice riddle. Here is an example of a riddle on an anchor:

> My twin points are joined together by crooked iron; with the wind
> I wrestle, with the depths of the sea I fight; I search out the midmost
> water, and I bite the very ground itself.

The next addition to the history of Anglo-Latin riddling is a collection of sixty-two riddles discovered in a monastery in the north Italian city of Bobbio near Genoa, subsequently described as the 'Berne Riddles'. Believed to have been written by an Irish monk by the name of Tullius in the seventh century, they represent the work of the first-ever Italian riddle-master of the Middle Ages. The subject matter of these enigmas is still very much concerned with folk themes, but though the collection was popular and was still being reprinted in the nineteenth century, the first major figure after Symphosius is unquestionably Aldhelm, the riddling saint.

St Aldhelm was an extraordinarily talented man. As well as being a brilliant scholar and theologian, the Abbot of Malmesbury and Bishop of Sherborne (one of the top dioceses in Wessex) was also an inveterate enigmatographer. Noted in the Venerable Bede's *Ecclesiastical History* as one of the fathers of the modern Church, he was an excellent musician, and his poems were greatly loved by Alfred. Indeed, the king himself related that in order to induce more people into church, Aldhelm would sing to them as they passed and drop sacred lyrics into his refrains. His riddles are one hundred in number and occur in the *Epistola ad Acircium*, a treatise on prosody written between AD 685 and 705 addressed to his friend Aldfrith ('Acircius'), King of Northumberland.

The subject matter of the riddles, which are again in hexameters, is much the same as that of Symphosius, with the exception that for the first time a Christian element is introduced together with a substantial amount of classical mythology and fable. The following is a simple folk-oriented riddle on wind:

> None can espy me, none lay hands on me;
> My rushing voice shrills swift through all the earth.
> I shatter oaks with harsh and hideous might,
> Yea, beat upon the skies, and sweep the fields.

In the wake of the literary saint came a succession of theological dignitaries, all of whom managed to find time between building churches, converting the heathen and studying the Scriptures to jot down some riddles to amuse, test and sometimes shock their sacred brethren. The erstwhile Archbishop of Canterbury, Tatwine, published forty hexameter riddles before he died on 30 July 734 in his own diocese, about a third of which were on religious topics. All are between four and sixteen lines long, and he employed an ingenious acrostic to preface his work in which the first letters of the answers to all forty riddles were contained:

> *Sub deno quater haec diverse enigmata torquens*
> *Stamine metrorum exstructor conserta retexit.*

(Twisting these riddles diversely in ten four times he who built them up revealed them by the thread of their metres.)

The first line contains the initial letters of the first words of all the riddles and the second line contains, in reverse order, the initial letters of the last word in their first lines!

Though by all literary yardsticks a competent poet, Tatwine's riddles are recorded as having been rather dull, but perhaps not so turgid as those of his successor in this brief history – Abbot

Eusebius of Wearmouth (d. 747) – who wrote sixty hexameter riddles which were published together with the archbishop's to complete the 'century' after the fashion of Symphosius.

The great Devonian missionary bishop Winfrid, later known as Boniface, took time off from his travels to pen twenty pithy enigmas, ten each on the moral virtues and vices, though again these are rather stilted. A great peripatetic, Boniface swept all before him in his religious fervour and showed the true light to large sections of pagan Germany and France in the time of Charles Martel (no doubt riddling as he went). A story is told of how he instantly won over a tribe of Hessian tree-worshippers by taking an axe to their sacred Oak of Jupiter, felling it in record time and somehow managing to make it fall in such a way that the trunk split into four neat sections as it hit the ground. A lifelong friend and correspondent of an expatriate Anglo-Saxon princess with the endearing name of Bugga, who had become a nun in Italy, Boniface eventually met his maker when he was murdered by a gang of recalcitrant pagans on 5 June 755 – a fountain is said to have sprung immediately from the spot.

The Venerable Bede himself is credited with having doodled out some riddles, though these are now generally held to be apocryphal, the manuscript indicating a hand much later than the great scholar's. The most notable of these works is generally known by its abbreviated title *Flores* and contains twelve original riddles together with direct quotations from other enigmatographers and a short colloquy. A rather clever riddle on a horse drawn by a pen will serve to illustrate the style:

> I am sitting above a horse which was not born, whose mother I hold in my hand.

Next came the ninth-century Lorsch manuscript of somewhat derivative riddles, and the works (mostly logographs) of the Byzantine school (*fl.* 950–1300), including Psellus and Christophorus of Mytilene. However, the last major enigmatographer in the Latin tradition of this period was Dr Claretus of Bohemia, who composed 150 mostly single-line folk-oriented enigmas in the fourteenth century, some of which were distinctly spicy whilst others, though more decent, tended to give the game away. Here is a rather longer one:

A layman comes with an iron spoon, shoves it in and opens up his mother; he salts her, and sews up her skin; then he takes his mother's children, grinds all their bones, and feeds his own children.

(The solution is 'a crop in a field'.)

Riddlers of the Hebrew Golden Age

The period from the middle of the tenth century to the end of the fifteenth century saw the flowering in Spain of the Golden Age of modern Hebrew literature. For it was at this time, under Moorish rule, that the Jewish community in the region of Andalusia, with its cultural centre at Cordova, suddenly burst forth with a host of talent in verse, song, prose and, most important for us, riddles. To Jews of the Middle Ages, whether threadbare children or venerated rabbis, the elaborate construction and telling of riddles was, as with the Ancient Greeks, a regular and accepted mode of table entertainment, and all the major Hebrew poets of this era composed enigmas and acrostics of great merit. Philosophical riddles appeared in monumental ethical works such as Solomon ibn Gabirol (aka Avicebron)'s eleventh-century *Choice of Pearls*, and some (e.g. the famous 'Who knoweth one?' number riddle for Passover Eve) even managed to find their way into the Jewish prayer-book.

Dunash ben Labrat (*c.*920–*c.*990) is generally regarded as being the founder of Spanish Hebrew poetry and the motivating power behind this hive of literary industry, for it was he who first introduced the Arabic metre into Hebrew verse, thus setting a trend that was to be much imitated throughout the Jewish world. He is particularly important in the history of enigmatography in that he stands midway between the Anglo-Latin school and the advent of riddling in the vernacular as represented in such works as the Anglo-Saxon *Exeter Book*. Very few of his riddles survive today, but to give an example of his style here is his enigma on a candle:

What weeps tears without an eye, and makes everything visible and does not see its own garment? At the time when it approaches death that which cuts off its head revives it.

Murdered by a jealous Muslim poet, his body was hidden under a fig tree and was only discovered some time later when suspicions were aroused by the amazing fruit the tree produced.

One of the most popular of the Hebrew riddles of this period was a long and highly technical grammatical treatise written by Abraham ibn Ezra (1089–1164), who is also believed to have used riddle-like phrases to conceal his unorthodox views on Judaism. Always a wanderer, his travels eventually led him to London and he is held to have been the inspiration for Robert Browning's poem 'Rabbi ben Ezra'. That the Victorian poet certainly knew of ibn Ezra's writings is evidenced by the fact that he incorporated one of the riddler's verses into his own 'Holy Cross Days' in 1854.

However, influential though the work of ibn Ezra may have been, it was his great contemporary Jehudah (or Judah) Halevi (c.1086–1141) who is variously credited with being not only the foremost Hebrew poet since the Bible and a religious philosopher of the first order, but is also held to be the Jewish enigmatographer *par excellence*. The German poet Heinrich Heine included a poem singing his praises in *Romancero* (1851), describing his abilities in nigh adulatory tones:

And Jehuda ben Halevy
Was not merely skill'd in reading,
But in poetry a master,
And himself a first-rate poet.

Yes, he was a first-rate poet,
Star and torch of his own age,
Light and beacon of his people,
Yes, a very wondrous mighty

Fiery pillar of all song,
That preceded Israel's mournful
Caravan as it was marching
Through the desert of sad exile.

Halevi's patron, that venerated poet and contemporary of Omar Khayyam, Moses ibn Ezra (who also wrote riddles), once described him as 'the star from Castile which will illuminate the world'. Born into a wealthy and learned family in Toledo, c.1086, Halevi studied medicine for some years at Lucena and later set up practice in Cordova, where he quickly became the town's foremost physician, leading a life of affluence and honour and writing poems and riddles in his spare moments. Halevi's riddles are contained in his *magnum opus* known as the *Cuzari* (or

Al-Khazari), described by some as the Song of Songs of modern Judaism. Over three hundred of his poems are included in the Jewish liturgy but to give an example of his enigmatic skill, here is his riddle on a needle:

> What is it that's blind with an eye in its head,
>> But the race of mankind its use cannot spare;
> Spends all its life in clothing the dead,
>> But always itself is naked and bare?

The last major Hebrew riddler of this period was an Italian friend and imitator of Dante Alighieri. Immanuel ben Solomon ben Jekuthiel, known as Immanuel of Rome (1260–c.1328), was by all accounts a cheerful young man (another friend of Dante's once described him as 'the happily laughing soul'). He led a profligate youth and there are innumerable tales of his womanizing, reading of 'improper books' and taste for Greek philosophy – a habit then considered totally unorthodox. One day, however, to his own bad fortune and posterity's good luck, Immanuel suddenly lost his entire wealth. In his subsequent wanderings he met a patron who encouraged him to collect his writings into a single book. But such was the Jewish community's opinion of their wayward bard that this anthology, in which are also included his riddles, was instantly banned as being too erotic and irreligious. Indeed, although a version appeared in 1535, another complete edition of the work, entitled *Mahberot Immanuel* ('Compositions of Immanuel'), did not appear until well into the eighteenth century.

Riddles for Everyman: the Vernacular

Riddles in the vernacular abound in the Middle Ages, which was a great time for the art as a whole. We hear of riddles in the bazaars of twelfth-century China, of the teasers of 'Ali the enigmatic', Fani and others in Turkey, and of countless examples both literary and oral in western Europe. As a result, it is only possible to scratch the surface of this huge treasury in a book of this size and mention just a few of the larger and more famous collections.

One of the most celebrated source-books of vernacular riddles and one of the most important general anthologies of early modern English literature is the Anglo-Saxon *Exeter Book*. Apart from the ninety-six (presumably originally one hundred) magnificent riddles contained therein, it also includes some of the major extant writings of the early Anglo-Saxon period: poems like 'The Wanderer', 'The Seafarer' and 'The Whale'.

Originally believed to have been the product of the eighth-century Anglo-Saxon poet Cynewulf's pen, the *Exeter Book* was probably written in the last quarter of the tenth century and was presented to Exeter Cathedral in 1072 by Leofric, the city's bishop. The riddles are of varying length (the average is 15 lines; the longest 108) and are on common natural topics (many being on weapons or pastoral/agricultural themes) in both folk and literary form. Most of the answers have now been largely agreed upon amongst the academics with the help of clues in the form of runes attached to some of the riddles in the manuscript.

Some of the riddles are mildly obscene but the majority are perfectly respectable, a good example being the following one on a plough:

> My beak is below, I burrow and nose
> Under the ground, I go as I'm guided
> By my master the farmer, old foe of the forest;
> Bent and bowed, at my back he walks,
> Forward pushing me over the field;
> Sows on my path where I've passed along.
> I came from the wood, a wagon carried me;
> I was fitted with skill, I am full of wonders.
> As grubbing I go, there's green on one side,
> But black on the other my path is seen.
> A curious prong pierces my back;
> Beneath me in front, another grows down
> And forward pointing is fixed to my head.
> I tear and gash the ground with my teeth,
> If my master steer me with skill from behind.

Whoever the author of the *Exeter Book* may have been, we can be sure that the composer of the Arabic literary masterpiece known as the *Maqamat* (or *Makamat*) was none other than the distinguished raconteur, poet, philologist and enigmatographer Al-Hariri. Born in the ancient city of Basra in Iraq, renowned for its learning and the famous school of Arabic grammar, Abu Muhammad Al-Qasim Al-Hariri (1054–1122) seemed destined to write riddles from an early age, for his lifelong occupation was as *sahib al Khabar* – chief of local intelligence. Noted for his ugliness and described as being 'of mean aspect', Al-Hariri (who none the less had three sons) is reputed to have informed an offended student: 'I am a man to be heard of, not seen.'

The *maqamat* (or collection of 'assemblies') was a literary form pioneered some years before, in which a narrator relates stories told by a wandering rhetorician as he journeys from town to town, living off the donations given by appreciative audiences who *assemble* to hear him. The idea of writing such a collection was suggested to Al-Hariri by his patron Anushirwan of Baghdad, who, having read his first tale (the forty-eighth in the final version), encouraged him to write more. On completion of forty Al-Hariri presented them at the court of his benefactor, but when he failed to produce others on the spot at Anushirwan's request he was accused of plagiarism, whereon he immediately returned home and wrote a further ten to complete the fifty that survive today. This appeared to stymie the critics and Al-Hariri quickly began to enjoy tremendous popularity, becoming greatly celebrated in his own lifetime and receiving acclaim from princes and poets alike. One contemporary of his, named Zamakhshari, even went as far as to say:

> I swear by God and His marvels,
> By the pilgrims' rite and their shrine:
> Hariri's *Assemblies* are worthy
> To be written in gold each line.

Written to please rather than instruct, the *Assemblies* do none the less contain a wealth of classical Arabic lore, including commentaries on the Koran, grammatical exercises, poetry and jokes, as well as riddles. And the enigmas themselves are of various kinds, involving plays on Arabic words, grammatical quizzes, etc. Here is an example of a more conventional type of riddle, taken from Chapter 42:

> What groom is it who weds, both in secret and openly, two sisters, and no offence at his wedlock is ever found? When waiting on one, he waits as well on the other eke: if husbands are partial, no such bias is seen in him. His attentions increase as the sweethearts are growing grey, and so does his largess: what a rare thing in married men!

to which the solution is 'kohl pencil'.

The continued success of the book – which has become a classic of the Arabic tongue second only to the Koran itself – is, apart from the overall excellence of the content, partly due to the fact that almost without exception the stories are, unusually for this period, entirely decent. Many translations and imitations have appeared both in the Orient and in European countries, though strangely a complete authoritative English version was not available until 1898.

Riddles also occur in other oriental literary classics in the vernacular dating from this period, perhaps the best-known being the *Shanamah*, or 'Book of Kings', of Persia. This beautifully illustrated book has been much admired over the years and stands as the major literary monument of Persian writing. Written by Firdusi (or Firdausi), a native of Tus in north-east Iran, the story, in 60,000 rhymed couplets, traces the history of the Persian people from their beginnings under Gayumarth until their conquest by the Arabs in the seventh century. Born *c.*950, its author, whose real name was Abul Qasim Mansur, took thirty years to complete the work and on presenting it to the Sultan Mahud the Great (998–1030) was shabbily treated. Instead of a piece of gold for every line as promised, he received silver, and was so incensed that he divided the money between a beer vendor and an attendant at a local baths before leaving the city in disgust. Heinrich Heine immortalized the story in his 'The Poet Ferdusi' and tells how:

Then his pilgrim staff he straightway
Grasp'd, and left at once the city,
And before the gate the dust he
From his very shoes rejected.

The riddles, mostly on cosmological themes, appear in the section where the hero Zal (son of Sam) is tested by Menucheich, Emperor of Iran. (Zal, of course, is well-versed in the art and passes the test with flying colours.) Here is an example on day and night:

There are two splendid horses, one black as pitch, the other of shining crystal; each runs ahead of the other but never catches it.

The *Shanamah* also inspired Matthew Arnold's poem 'Sohrab and Rustum' (1853).

Appendix: Apollonius of Tyre and the Incest Riddle

No account of riddling of this period, whether in Latin or the vernacular, would be complete without some reference to the story of Apollonius of Tyre and the evil king Antiochus. One of the best-known romances of the Middle Ages and the Renaissance, the tale appeared in over a hundred different Latin manuscript editions, the oldest of which dates from the ninth century, although allusions to previous accounts seem to indicate an ancestry more venerable still, perhaps dating back to a Hellenistic novel in the manner of Xenophon. (For Shakespeare's version see Chapter 3, page 48.)

Simply put, the plot is basically as follows: King Antiochus has committed incest with his daughter and wants to prevent her marrying anyone else. To this end he decides to test each royal suitor with the following riddle:

> The branch's leaf is like the root.
> The father eats the mother's fruit.

Success would guarantee the lady's hand, failure the suitor's death. After many gory challenges, King Apollonius of Tyre sails into town to try his hand and solves the riddle easily but is justifiably upset:

> '. . . This riddle is unfair.
> It brings all guessers shame and care.
> If its dark words are plainly said,
> They mean you take your child to bed.

> 'You are the root, your child the tree.
> In mortal sin through her you be.
> Your child inherits the fleshly act
> Her mother did in marriage pact.'

Needless to say the bad king Antiochus is enraged at being so exposed and seeks to murder Apollonius, who heads off on a world cruise forthwith with Antiochus's hitman Talliarchus hot on his heels. However, shipwreck brings the luckless Apollonius to Pentapolis where he eventually marries the king's daughter, Luciana. Hearing some time later that Antiochus and his daughter have died, Apollonius and his queen set sail homewards, but Luciana dies in childbirth at sea and in his grief Apollonius leaves the baby Tarsiana to be brought up at Tarsus and goes into self-imposed exile in Egypt until his daughter's wedding day. Returning ten years later and being shown Tarsiana's supposed grave, the poor fellow in his misery sails to his home town of Tyre to die. However, a storm drives him to Mytilene where his daughter had in fact been taken in slavery by pirates and has become well known for her singing. Sent to entertain the noble visitor, the girl refuses to accept his money until he either cheers up or answers a number of riddles such as the following:

> Downy inside, and smooth to the air,
> Inside my breast I wear my hair.
> From hand to hand I go in play.
> When men go eat, outside I stay.

to which Apollonius gives the solution 'ball'. The king guesses all the riddles but Tarsiana is so moved by his sadness that she hugs him. Apollonius throws her off and, upset, she recounts her whole unhappy life, on hearing which Apollonius discovers that she is his daughter. Sailing home in their subsequent joy, they happen upon Luciana who had been washed ashore, still alive, at Ephesus, and the whole family live happily ever after.

CHAPTER THREE
The Renaissance and Beyond

After the passionate outpourings of the Golden Age of Hebrew literature, the finely honed enigmas of the Anglo-Latin poets and their successors and the superb forays into riddling in the vernacular by the likes of Al-Hariri and the author of the *Exeter Book*, the opening to the great renaissance of fine art and architecture of the sixteenth and seventeenth centuries went off at first like a damp squib for the history of enigmatography. Indeed, it was a mystery in itself when the first stirrings of renewed interest did manifest themselves, coming as they did not from the formerly intensive breeding grounds of enigmatic composition but rather from the pens of a small number of German scribes writing in Latin. Once begun, however, the great machinery of enigmatography soon got into gear and cruised massively and with even greater finesse through the reigns of Henry VIII to Cromwell, past Caxton and Columbus to the Reformation, Lepanto and Shakespeare. A new generation of master riddlers would soon emerge and the subtle wit of Cervantes, Malatesti, Straparola and the anonymous English collections would once again tease the public imagination to the limits of its collective endurance with this maddening yet delightful literary exercise.

The German Enigma

In the wake of such early riddling classics as the contest between Wolfram and Klingsor in the medieval *Wartburgkrieg* and the closely guarded enigmas of the famous 'Meistersingers', the first major collection of riddles to emerge in this period was the anonymous German anthology culled from many sources and known as the *Strassburger Rätselbuch* (1505).

After this came a long string of German Protestant academics

composing literary enigmas in Latin. The first of these, Ludovi-
cus Helmbold (1532–98), was a teacher and minister of the church
in Muhlhausen in Thuringia and published a hundred rather
pedestrian riddles under the title *Aenigmatum centuria*. Next,
William of Orange's lawyer, Johannes Lorichius Secundus (also
known as Hadamerius from his birthplace near Koblenz), published an enormous three-volume collection entitled *Aenigmatum
libri tres* in 1545, which was followed twenty years later by the
Emblematum et aenigmatum libellus of the celebrated emblematist
Hadrian Junius.

However, though Junius was regarded by many as being the
most distinguished writer of Latin riddles in northern Europe of
this period, it is perhaps his successor, Nicolaus Reusner, Rector
of Jena University (where years later another enigmatographer,
Schiller, was to further the art), who is best known today. Not
only did Reusner compose riddles on his own account but he also
compiled an enormous collection, *Aenigmatographia*, in which he
preserved for posterity many examples that would otherwise
undoubtedly have been lost to us today. Here is the riddle for
smoke taken from his volume *Aenigmata*, published in the last
year of his life (1602):

> *Lacryma multa mihi, sed nulla est causa doloris,*
> *Coeli affecto vitam, sed gravis aer obest.*

(Many are the tears I give but there is no cause for grief. I strive for
life in the sky, but the weighty air engulfs me.)

A year earlier, 120 enigmas from the hand of Johannes Lauter-
bach (1531–93), a teacher in Heilbronn, appeared for the first time
in print, and later yet another teacher, Johannes Buchler of
Gladbach in north Germany, found time between lessons and
marking homework to put together an equally popular collection. This book, whose abbreviated title is *Gnomologia*, was first
issued in 1602 and contained a variety of folklore pieces including
proverbs and songs as well as riddles. Joachim Camerarius of
Papenberg also wrote some riddles at this time and 420 enigmas
were published by Huldrich Therander in 1605, though most of
these are merely German versions of older Latin originals.

Riddling in England

The passion for riddling, ever strong in medieval Britain, grew apace during the Renaissance and many collections circulated during this period, worthy both as works of literature in their own right and for the influence they had on the great poets, playwrights and thinkers of the day – the most notable of whom was, of course, the bard of Stratford-upon-Avon himself: William Shakespeare.

Shakespeare would undoubtedly have made the acquaintance of the works of the great riddle-masters of the past and those of his own time, and there are innumerable allusions to riddles and riddling in his plays. Lysander 'riddles very prettily' in *A Midsummer Night's Dream*; 'riddling confession finds but riddling shrift' for Romeo in *Romeo and Juliet*; and a rather grim enigma also appears in the gravediggers' scene of *Hamlet* (Act V, Scene 1) thus:

> *First Clown:* What is he that builds stronger than either the mason, the shipwright or the carpenter?
> *Second Clown:* The gallows-maker; for that frame outlives a thousand tenants.

That Shakespeare had certainly read the *History of Apollonius of Tyre* in some shape or form is evidenced by his dramatization of the basic plot in his play *Pericles*. In fact, the choice of name for his continuity character, Gower, seems to suggest that it was the version of the tale in John Gower's *Confessio Amantis* (1390) that had fired his imagination. Be that as it may, the substance of the plot is much the same, though Shakespeare's version – unlike, say, the Spanish *El Libro di Apolonio* – lacks the sequence of riddles when Apollonius (Pericles in Shakespeare) confronts his long-lost daughter Tarsiana (Shakespeare's Marina). However, his treatment of the key Antiochus riddle is masterful:

> I am no viper, yet I feed
> On mother's flesh which did me breed.
> I sought a husband, in which labour
> I found that kindness in a father.
> He's father, son, and husband mild;
> I mother, wife and yet his child:
> How they may be, and yet in two,
> As you will live, resolve it you.
>
> (*Pericles*, Act I, Scene 1, 65–72)

Riddling was practised in all walks of life under the Tudors, from the lowly peasant with his fireside jokes and pleasantries to the razor-sharp wit of the court *littérateurs* – even the ill-fated Sir Thomas More is said to have penned a few enigmas at this time.

The metaphysical poet John Donne alludes to the power of the enigmatic art when he describes the complexities of the soul in his *Sermons*: 'Poor intricated soul! Riddling, perplexed, labyrinthine soul!'; and Thomas Campion in 'Winter Nights' talks of filling the long evenings:

This time doth well dispense
    With lovers' long discourse;
Much speech hath some defence,
    Though beauty no remorse.
All things do not all things well;
    Some measures comely tread,
Some knotted riddles tell,
    Some poems smoothly read.

And 'labyrinthine' the riddle had certainly become at the hands of some of the finer exponents of the art with the massive upsurge in learning that the Renaissance brought with it across the mainland of Europe. However, a certain earthiness can still be found in many of the enigmas of this period. This was, after all, the time of the riddles of Stigliani and Straparola, and even official court riddlers could still get away with the occasional uncensored ribaldry, as the following exchange between the far-from-prudish Henry VIII and his jester Will Sommers testifies:

'Now tell me,' says Will, 'if you can, what it is, that being born without life, head, lip or eye, yet doth run roaring through the world till it die?'
'This is a wonder,' quod the king, 'and no question. I know it not.'
'Why,' quod Will, 'it is a fart.'
At this the king laughed heartily and was exceeding merry. . . .
                (from R. Armin, *Foole upon Foole*, 1600)

The first riddle book ever printed in the English language was *The Demaundes Joyous*, produced by Wynkyn de Worde in 1511. Essentially a selective translation of a French book (by an anonymous author) known as *Demandes joyeuses en manière de quodlibets*, published at the end of the previous century, it contains a series of fifty-four questions prefaced by the word 'Demaunde' and followed by the solutions; it is quite short, being only six pages in all. Some of the riddles are mildly obscene (though the worst have been edited out by the English printer), and some are rather dull, being just questions testing one's knowledge of the Bible. None the less this little book, originally published in the reign of Henry VIII, has remained immensely popular over the years. Here is a short example of the kind of riddle it contains:

What thing is it, the less it is the more it is dread?

to which the answer is 'a bridge'.

Another popular collection of the sixteenth century was again anonymous and went by the title of *The Riddles of Heraclitus and Democritus* (1598), being printed by Arnold Hatfield. It will be remembered that Heraclitus was for long regarded as having been the arch-riddler of pre-Socratic philosophy and this collection, though certainly in no way connected with the work of the ancient Greek seer, gained a certain kudos from using his name in the title. There are sixty riddles in all, of varying lengths and metres, on subjects ranging from animals to household objects – like the following riddle on a pound of candles:

On an evening as colde as colde might bee,
    With frost and haile, and pinching weather,
Companions about three times three
    Lay close in a pound together:
Yet one after one they took a heate
    And died that night, all in a sweate.

The little-known poet Humphrey Gifford (*fl.*1580) also produced a commendable collection of eighteen enigmas at this time which were published at the end of a volume of his verse entitled *Posie of Gillowflowers* (1580), a sample from which can be found in Part 2, pages 131–2. And the somewhat more famous poet and emblematist George Wither is also credited with having composed a number of enigmas, notably a collection entitled *The Dark Lantern* (1653), which heading continues in the following vein: '. . . containing a dim Discoverie in Riddles, Parables, and Semi-Riddles, intermixed with Cautions, Rememberances, and Predictions, as they were promiscuously represented to their Author, November 3, 1652 about midnight'. Other collections creating interest at this time were *Sphynx Thebanus* (1664) and *Wit's Academy* (1656), reputed to have been the work of Ben

Jonson. Sir Thomas Wyatt also seems to have turned his hand to fashioning a few riddles as the following verse on a gun bears witness:

Vulcan begat me; Minerva me taught:
Nature, my mother; Craft nourisht me year by year:
Three bodies are my foode: my strength is naught.
Anger, wrath, waste, and noise are my children dear.
Guess, my friend, what I am: and how I am wraught:
Monster of sea, or of land, or of elsewhere.
Know me and use me: and may thee defend:
And if I be thine enemy, I may thy life end.

(from *Tottel's Miscellany*, 1557)

During this period a number of volumes of enigmas appeared with titles that varied on the theme of 'A Book of Merry Riddles' (in various spellings). These are all believed to draw on a rather salacious collection called *A Hundred Merry Riddles*, produced by William Rastell, which appeared in about 1530. A cleaned-up edition of this book, containing only seventy-six riddles, was extremely popular in Shakespeare's own time and may well have been the 'Book of Riddles' that Slender has lost in *The Merry Wives of Windsor*:

Slender: . . . How now, Simple, where have you been? I must wait on myself, must I? You have not the book of Riddles about you, have you?

Simple: Book of Riddles? Why, did you not lend it to Alice Shortcake upon All-hallowmas last, a fortnight afore Michaelmas?

(Act I, Scene 1, 181–6)

Another important collection that survives from this time is the one now commonly referred to as *The Holme Riddles*, an anthology of over 140 enigmas collected by the Randle Holme family of Chester. There were four Randle Holmes (b. 1571, 1601, 1627 and 1659) and the manuscript is written in three different hands. Many of the riddles, which are on the usual folk themes and are sometimes obscene, can be traced back to other sources, but one particularly striking and original example is the following on a rose-bud:

there is a thing wch hath five chins 2 hath beards 2 hath none, & one it hath but half an one.

(The rose's outward green leaves are both jagged and plain.)

The Italian School

Meanwhile in Italy enigmatography had reached a degree of sophistication hitherto undreamt of. Immanuel of Rome, Dante's riddling Jewish friend, had set the pace with his *Mahberot*, and following in his wake, all the major scribes of the day sharpened up their quill pens and set to, it being quite the thing to be known to be engaged in this high-society fad in one's spare time. It is said that Dante himself wrote riddles, as did Petrarch; and the talented Boccaccio included a number of acrostics in his unfinished work *Amorosa Visione*. Even the extraordinarily versatile Leonardo da Vinci is credited with some enigmatic pronouncements, and seven salacious enigmas flowed from the hand of that renowned man of letters and namesake of Francesco Griffo's excellent seriffed typeface (in which this book is set), Cardinal Pietro Bembo (1470–1547). The great astronomer Galileo Galilei also wrote a number of highly acceptable riddles such as the following on a riddle:

> Mostro son io più strano, è più difforme
>   Che l'Arpia, la Sirena, o la Chimera;
>   Nè in terra, in aria, in acqua è alcuna fiera,
>   Ch'abbia di membra così varie forme.
> Parte a parte non ho che sia conforme,
>   Più che s'una sia bianca, o l'altra nera;
>   Spesso di cacciator dietro ho una schiera,
>   Che de' miei piè van rintracciando l'orme.
> Nelle tenebre oscure è il mio soggiorno;
>   Che se dall'ombre al chiaro lume passo,
>   Tosto l'alma da me sen fugge, come
> Sen fugge il sogno all'apparir del giorno,
>   E le mie membra disunite lasso,
>   E l'esser perdo con la vita, e'l nome.

(I am a monster, stranger and more alien than the Harpy, the Siren or the Chimera. Neither on land, in the air or in the sea is there a beast whose limbs can have so many shapes; no one piece of me conforms with another, anymore than if one is white, the other is black. A band of hunters often follows behind me looking for the tracks made by my feet. I inhabit the darkest places, and if I pass from the shadows into bright light my soul quickly slips away with the coming of the day and my tired limbs fall away, and I lose my being with my life and with my name.)

The composition of riddles in Latin continued to flourish during this period. Lilio Gregorio Giraldi's *Aenigmatum ex antiquis* . . . (1551) collected together in one book all the enigmas from classical antiquity known at that time, and Julius Caesar Scaliger (*Poetices*, 1561; *Poemata*, 1591), whose complete works run into over 1,000 pages, is credited with having written more Latin enigmas than any other Italian – in his own words '*plurima fecimus nos*' – a good example being this specimen on a plough from *Poemata*:

Ore gero gladium, matrisque in pectore condo
  Ut mox, qua nunc sunt mortua, viva colas.
Dux meus a tergo caudamque trahens retrahensque
  Hasta non me ut eam verberat ast alios.

(I carry a sword in my mouth, and I bury it in my mother's breast so that soon you may cultivate, alive, what is now dead. My leader from behind me sticks a tail on me and drags it back and forth, and lashes not me but others, in order to beat her.)

However, it was with riddles in the vernacular that the Italians really excelled. One of the best and certainly the most prolific Italian enigmatographer of the sixteenth century was the blacksmith-riddler Giulio Cesare Croce (1550–1609). Born at San Giovanni in Persiceto in northern Italy, Croce finally settled in Bologna, siring no less than fourteen children and giving birth to an incredible 478 literary works of various kinds. He is especially noteworthy in that not only are the riddles in his two major collections – *Notte sollazzevole di cento enigmi* . . . (1599) and *Seconde notte* . . . (1601) – perhaps the most original of his time, but they are also exceptional in being almost entirely 'decent'. Nearly all the other riddlers of Renaissance Italy included among their works subjects of a highly obscene nature. Indeed, thirty-six of Stigliani's forty-three octaves and sonnets are still deemed too foul to reprint even today. Here is Croce's riddle on the earth:

Sospesa in aria stò, nè tocco nulla,
  E circondata son di lumi intorno,
  Hor di novo mi vesto, hora son brulla,
  E al caldo, al freddo stò la notte, e'l giorno,
  Ogn'un di calpestạrmi si trastulla,
  Fino alle bestie mi fan danno, e scorno,
  E tai tesori ascondo nel mio seno,
  Che chi gli trova fò felice a pieno.

(I am suspended in the air, I touch nothing, and I am surrounded by lights. Now I dress myself afresh, and now I am naked, and I am in the heat and the cold, by night and by day. Everyone amuses himself by trampling upon me, even the animals abuse and scorn me, and yet I have such treasures hidden in my bosom that he who finds them I can make full of happiness.)

Gifted writers such as Cenni (another riddling blacksmith) and the pseudonymous author of seventy-one riddling sonnets known as 'Madonna Daphne' must for reasons of space be passed over quickly here. However, no account of riddling in Renaissance Italy could be complete without giving due consideration to the superb irreverent creations of Giovanni Francesco Straparola. Despite the banning of his *Facetious Nights* and the 'castrated' versions that appeared following it, this book was none the less tremendously successful and went into twenty editions in as many years (Boccaccio had to wait fifty years before the eighteenth edition of *The Decameron* appeared), influencing many subsequent riddle-masters and supplying fables to be retold later by such major figures as Perrault and Molière. Though many of the seventy-four uproarious tales derive from Boccaccio, the *Gesta Romanorum, Thousand and One Nights*, Morlini's *Novellae* and ancient Sanskrit yarns, some – notably the world-famous story of Belphegor – are the product of Straparola's own pen. Perhaps most memorable of all his creations is the fairy tale of *Puss in Boots*, reworked for posterity by Perrault, the Brothers Grimm and the German poet Tieck. Stories taken from the *Facetious Nights* also appear in Painter's *Palace of Pleasure* (1566) and it was much drawn on by the versatile riddler Alexandre Sylvain. Not all Straparola's riddles were rude, of course, as the following example on a football attests:

Dead to men I seem to be,
Yet surely breath there is in me;
Cruel is my fate, I trow,
Buffeted now high, now low.
But assaults of fist and heel
Vex me not, for naught I feel.
Blameless I midst all my woes,
Yet find all men my bitter foes,
Backwards, forwards, urged and driven,
Soaring high from earth to heaven.

Moving on to the seventeenth century, the first enigmatographer of note – or perhaps it would be more accurate to say notoriety – was another riddling scandal-monger: Tommaso Stigliani. Born in 1573, Stigliani was employed in the court of Charles Emmanuel I and seems to have spent a large part of his spare time composing outrageous enigmas which were published (including the thirty-six unrepeatable ones) in the still prohibited *Rime* (1605). A slightly cleaner version appeared as *Canzoniero* in 1623.

Another wayward riddler of this period was the Franciscan friar Francesco Moneti. Perhaps best known as one of the greatest humorous satirical poets of his age, Moneti is reputed to have possessed a distinct lack of the humility and brotherly love required of one of his calling. Born in 1635, Antonio Moneti changed his Christian name as a mark of respect when he entered the order at the age of sixteen. However, such was his reputation for writing scurrilous verse that when a lampoon appeared on the death of Pope Clement X (1669) Moneti was immediately seized and imprisoned for nearly twelve months as being the most likely author (he was in fact innocent on this occasion).

His riddles are contained in three books published around 1699 which overlap somewhat, perhaps the most complete edition being *Apollo ennimatico*, which contains 150 riddles in the form of octaves, sestinas and quatrains on everyday topics such as candles and salt, with a sprinkling of more abstract subjects like vice, truth and death.

Michelangelo Buonarroti the Younger (1568–1646), grand-nephew of the artist and a poet in his own right, wrote seventy-one very 'decent' riddles, and a very large anonymous collection known as the *Genoa University Manuscript* also dates from this period.

However, the unquestioned master of Italian seventeenth-century riddling was Antonio Malatesti. Born in Florence in 1610 and later to become a member of the distinguished Accademia degli Apatisti, Malatesti was a friend of the poet Lorenzo Lippi and features in the latter's classic poem *Malmatile Racquistato* as 'Amostante Latoni' (which is an anagram of the riddler's name). His play *La Tina* was dedicated to Milton (who is supposed to have met Malatesti whilst travelling in Italy) but it is for his riddle collection *La Sfinge* – in three parts (1640, 1643 and 1683) – that he is best remembered today. This book inspired many subsequent riddlers and though some of the subject-matter can hardly be classified as altogether proper, it certainly cannot be termed vulgar. In total the three parts contain 269 sonnets, 57 octaves and 66 quatrains, a rather limited sample of which is included in Part 2 (see pages 142–3), though the riddle on a mirror warrants inclusion here to give an impression of the master's touch:

> *Chi vuol vedere quel che fuggir non può,*
> *venga venga una volta innanzi a me,*
> *che s'avrà gli occhi e la ragion con sè,*
> *conoscerà quel ch'io gli mostrerò.*
> *In virtù dell'argento il tutto fo*
> *non avend'io religïon, nè fè;*
> *ignudo mostro il corpo com'egli è,*
> *se dal fiato dell'uom panni non ò.*
> *Nè m'importa, se un brutto in odio m'à,*
> *mentre un bello si val di mia virtù,*
> *perchè chiara i'vo'dir la verità.*
> *Piccola o grande vaglio meno e più;*
> *ma se non fusse la fragilità,*
> *varrei più, che non val tutto il Perù.*

(He who wants to see what is escaping, and cannot, let him come once first to me, for if he has got his eyes and his reason with him, he will know what I will show him. I do everything in the virtue of silver, having no religion or faith; I show the body, naked as it is, if I am not clothed by the breath of man. Nor does it matter to me, if I am held in hatred by someone ugly whilst a beautiful person values my worth, because I will speak the truth clearly. The small or the large I consider less and more; but if it were not for my fragility, I would be worth more than the whole of Peru.)

The celebrated essayist Michel de Montaigne (1533–92) is credited with having declared:

> I have a backward and torpid mind; the least cloud stops its progress. I have never, for example, found a riddle easy enough for me to solve.

However, this is not to say that French enigmatography of this period was initially of a particularly complicated kind. In fact, the folk-riddles of the highly successful *Les Adevineaux amoureux*, produced by an anonymous author in 1478, owe much of their popularity to the simplicity of their presentation, as this enigma on lice, fingers and eyes testifies:

> Two who run and ten who chase them, two who look on, and one who puts them to death.

Another bestselling riddle book from this period was the original of Wynkyn de Worde's *Demaundes Joyous*. As mentioned earlier, de Worde's edition was really nothing more than a translation and adaptation (omitting some of the more obscene riddles) of an anonymous collection of enigmas entitled *Demandes joyeuses en manière de quodlibets*, printed some time before 1500. The original, however, contained eighty-seven *demandes* whilst de Worde's has only fifty-four.

Two spoof riddles occur in Rabelais's *Gargantua* (1534), whilst Chapter 19 of *Pantagruel* (1532) depicts a dumb-show exchange of rebuses between the witty buffoon Panurge and the English philosopher Thaumast. And in Chapter 11 of the so-called 'Fifth Book' of the series Panurge and company are arrested by Clawpuss, Archduke of the Furrycats, a race of terrible creatures that eat little children and feed on marble stones. From his seat of justice, the monster demands an answer to the following riddle:

> A pretty creature, young and fair and slender,
> Conceived, without a sire, a swarthy son
> And bore him painlessly, the little tender
> Suckling, although his birth was a strange one.
> For, like a viper, through her side he bored
> Impatiently, a truly hideous thing,
> And then o'er hill and valley boldly soared,
> Riding the air, or o'er land journeying;

Which drove the Friend of Wisdom out of his mind,
For he had thought him of the human kind.

After some humming and hawing Panurge eventually comes up with the solution, which is a black weevil born from a white bean. (Pythagoras – 'Friend of Wisdom' equals 'philosopher' – believed it to have received a human soul from somewhere by metempsychosis.)

Tabourot des Accords's study of rebuses and other kinds of puzzles, entitled *Les Bigarrures du Seigneur des Accords*, also appeared at about this time (1582) and was well received. As well as examples of the pictorial form the book also included chapters on literary and even musical rebuses. A good example is the following lover's riddle:

comme ♡ ♡ *ay-s-me iusques*

which reads *deux coeurs en un coeur* and *s'entre-aymer, iusques à la fin comme au commencement* ('two hearts in one heart' and 'to love one another the same at the end as at the beginning').

Charles Fontaine is credited with a collection of *Odes, énigmes et épigrammes* dating from 1557, but it seems that the only French riddler of any renown in the sixteenth century was Alexandre Sylvain (in reality the Belgian poet and enigmatographer Alexander van den Bussche), whose *Cinquante aenigmes françoises* appeared in 1582. These riddles draw mainly on Italian sources, such as Straparola, and are generally of sonnet form. Here is an example on an oyster:

> *Ie n'ay ny pieds, ny mains, ny teste, mais un corps,*
> *Qui est tousiours armé d'une armure bien forte*
> *Qui me sert de rampart, de fenestre, & de porte,*
> *Et par fois est ouverte à ceux qui par dehors*
> *Guettent: pour me manger, car plus que moy sont forts.*
> *Mais pour mieux leur monstrer combien celà m'importe*
> *Ie les retiens captifs, & prins de telle sorte*
> *Que malgré leur effort souvent demeurent morts.*
> *Ie ne les mange point, car ce qu'est ma viande*
> *Est si tres delicat qu'à peine se peut voir,*
> *En fin ie suis mangé tant ma misere est grande,*
> *Qui me sçaura nommer fera bien son devoir.*

(I have neither feet, nor hands, nor head, but only a body, which is always protected by very strong armour that serves as rampart, window and door, and is sometimes opened to those who are outside lying in wait: to eat me, for they are stronger than me. But in order to show them how much I resent this, I keep them captive and prisoner so that in spite of all their efforts they often die. But I do not eat them, because the kind of food I eat is so dainty that you can hardly see it. In the end, though, I am eaten and my misery is great. He who can name me will have performed his task well.)

The following century saw the publication in 1694 of a remarkable treatise on enigmatography entitled *La philosophie des images énigmatiques*. Composed by the Jesuit historian and heraldic scholar Claude-François Menestrier, this thorough study discusses the background and significance of most varieties of riddle from oracles to hieroglyphics and even includes a section of sample enigmas of each sort, a selection of which is included in the anthology in Part 2 (see pages 143–5).

This period also saw the composition of the poet Boileau's famous riddle on the flea:

Du repos des Humains implacable Ennemie,
J'ay rendu mille Amans envieux de mon sort;
Je me repais de sang, et je trouve ma vie
Dans les bras de celui qui recherche ma mort.

(Implacable enemy of human rest, I have made a thousand lovers jealous of my lot; I feast on blood, and find my life in the arms of those who seek my death.)

This fine enigma was communicated to Boileau's friend, the advocate Brossette, in a letter of 29 September 1703, Boileau claiming it to be his first-ever literary work, as he had composed it around 1652 when he was only seventeen.

Riddling questions can be found in *Les Aventures de Télémaque* (1699), the best-known work of Fénélon, Archbishop of Cambrai (1651–1715), and another popular collection dating from this time is Abbé Cotin's *Recueil des énigmes de ce temps*, containing over a hundred riddles, including a number on the riddle itself.

Cervantes and Riddling in Spain

Travelling further south we find the riddle in fine fettle on the Iberian peninsula. The tradition of *preguntas* (a kind of riddling question in rhyme) was already well established by the time of the publication of Spain's first important collection of riddles: Luis Escobar's *Respuetas a las cuatrocientas preguntas* (1545). This was followed by Sebastian de Horozco's *Cancionero*, containing many excellent enigmas both respectable and obscene. And in 1581 Sylvain appeared again, this time in the guise of Alexandro Sylvano, with a collection of forty riddles entitled *Quarenta aenigmas en lengua espannola*.

However, dominating the seventeenth century – master of the riddle as well as every other aspect of Spanish literature of this period – is the phenomenal character of Miguel de Cervantes Saavedra, author of the masterpiece *Don Quixote*. Some particularly notable examples of his riddling skill occur in Book 6 of the pastoral epic *La Galatea*, written before *Don Quixote* in 1585, in which the heroine (after whom the book is named) is engaged in an outdoor exchange of wits with her friends. The riddling session, however, is cut short prematurely by the sound of a struggle between a person attempting suicide and some shepherds on the banks of a nearby river. This riddle on a riddle is perhaps best representative of Cervantes's style (others can be found in Part 2, page 119–21):

Dark 'tis, yet very clear,
Containing infinite variety,
Encumbering us with truths,
Which are at length declared.
'Tis sometimes of a jest produced,
At others of high fancy.
And it is wont defiance to create,
Of airy matters treating.

Any man its name may know,
Even to little children,
Many there are, and masters have
In different ways.
There is no old woman it embraces not,
With of these ladies, one
At times in good odour,
This tires, that satisfies.

Wise ones there be who overwatch
Sensations to extract.
Some run wild
The more they watch o'er it.
Such is foolish, and such curious,
Such easy, such complex,
Yet, be it something, be it nought,
Reveal to me what the said thing may be?

It is perhaps sad to think that Cervantes, who did not compose *Don Quixote* until he was fifty years old and whose works were enormously popular in his own lifetime, should none the less die a pauper – another riddle perhaps.

CHAPTER FOUR
Revival and Decline

As every schoolboy knows (and every schoolgirl too), the eighteenth century was the great *Wendepunkt* of modern European history. Hard on the heels of the glittering grand monarchies of Louis XIV and Frederick the Great of Prussia came the 'Age of Revolutions', when justice was meted out to the spendthrift aristocracy, the starving masses received their due and the yoke of a medieval form of government was cast off for ever. This was the period of the American War of Independence (1775–83) and the French Revolution (1789–99), of Paine and Rousseau and the Romantic Movement that drew its ideals from them, and of the great satirists Pope and Swift. And, quite apart from 'Madame Guillotine', it was also a time of great advances in technology, particularly in the media, with broadsheets and magazines reaching the general public to an extent undreamt of only a short while before. In company with the polemics, lampoons, news items and poems, one of the literary forms that took advantage of the widespread dissemination of the printed word was the riddle, which was already gaining a renewed upsurge of interest in the contemporary enthusiasm for riddle ballads collected later by Sir Walter Scott and others in Great Britain.

Through the influence of the beautifully worked creations of Schiller in Germany, Swift in England and many of the Italian enigmatographers (notably Catone l'Uticense Lucchese), riddling once again became a major public entertainment and private pastime, and fashionable folk fairly buzzed with the latest enigmas from the new breed of virtuosi. Riddlemania seemed to have permeated all levels of society, but particular impact during this age of turmoil came from the higher intellectual strata – even the great French *philosophe* François Voltaire being credited with some erudite riddling verses. And his equally great contemporary, the luminary Jean Jacques Rousseau, managed to take time off from influencing the course of world history to pen a few *énigmes* such as the following on a portrait, published in 1776:

Enfant de l'Art, Enfant de la Nature,
Sans prolonger les jours j'empêche de mourir:
Plus je suis vrai, plus je fais d'imposture,
Et je deviens trop jeune à force de vieillir.

(Child of Art, Child of Nature, without prolonging life, I prevent death: the truer I am, the more false I appear, and I become too young as age creeps on.)

However, with the riddle-masters of the eighteenth century the sun of Western enigmatography had reached its zenith and though commendable work continued to be published in the following decades and beyond, the light of this particular form of literary wit had begun to fade on the popular imagination and never again would public enthusiasm for such prankish metaphors wax so great.

Sturm und Drang . . . *and Riddles*

Johann Wolfgang von Goethe took an active interest in the riddle form and a number of witty enigmas by this literary giant were circulated to friends between 1802 and 1827. But it was with Goethe's friend and co-director (along with Herder) of the German *Sturm und Drang* Movement in European Romanticism – Friedrich von Schiller – that the literary riddle arguably achieves its highest expression of all time.

Born in 1759, Schiller stands in the front rank of German playwright-poets of this period and was also highly esteemed as an historian, succeeding to the chair of History at Jena University in the very year that the Paris mob was laying waste the Bastille prison. S. T. Coleridge rendered his play *Wallenstein* into English and his riddles still carry much of their delightful mystery in translation. Here is an example taken from a miscellaneous collection entitled *Parabeln und Rätsel* (1803) (see also Part 2, pages 168–72):

A bird it is, whose rapid motion
    With eagle's flight divides the air;
A fish it is, and parts the ocean,
    That bore a greater monster ne'er;

An elephant it is, whose rider
　　On his broad back a tower has put:
'Tis like the reptile base, the spider,
　　Whenever it extends its foot;
And when, with iron tooth projecting,
　　It seeks its own life-blood to drain,
On footing firm, itself erecting,
　　It braves the raging hurricane.

The solution is 'a ship'.

Many of these enigmas had already had a public airing in another of Schiller's plays, *Turandot* (1802), translated from the original Italian creation of Carlo Gozzi. In order to keep the audiences guessing, Schiller would depart from Gozzi's three basic riddles and introduce different ones at every performance. Gozzi's original riddles were:

> Who is the creature which belongs to every country, is a friend of the entire world, and does not tolerate its equal? Who is the mother that gives birth to her children, and devours them when they grow up? What is the tree whose leaves are white on one side and black on the other?

to which the solutions are, respectively, 'the sun', 'the sea' and 'the year'.

Swift and the Enigma in England

Meanwhile in England interest in riddling had recommenced with increased vigour. Notable public figures such as William Pitt the Younger (1759–1806), Richard Whately (1787–1863) who was Archbishop of Dublin and former Professor of Political Economy at Oxford University, and the Whig statesman Charles James Fox (1749–1806) all composed enigmas. The pastoral poet William Cowper even managed to scratch out the following riddle in July 1780 between his many fits of despondency:

> I am just two and two, I am warm, I am cold,
> And the parent of numbers that cannot be told.
> I am lawful, unlawful – a duty, a fault,
> I am often sold dear, good for nothing when bought;
> An extraordinary boon, and a matter of course,
> And yielded with pleasure when taken by force.

which when printed in *The Gentleman's Magazine* some years later (December 1806) received this riddling reply:

A riddle by Cowper
Made me swear like a trooper;
But my anger, alas! was in vain;
  For, remembering the bliss
  Of beauty's soft Kiss,
I now long for such riddles again.

Another notable contribution at this time was by the poet Catherine Maria Fanshawe (1765–1834) who wrote the famous 'A Riddle on the Letter H', once mistakenly credited to Lord Byron. Here is the 'amended' version with the now generally accepted alteration to the opening line:

'Twas whispered in heaven, 'twas muttered in hell,
And echo caught faintly the sound as it fell;
On the confines of earth 'twas permitted to rest,
And the depth of the ocean its presence confessed . . .
Yet in shade let it rest, like a delicate flower,
Ah, breathe on it softly, – it dies in an hour.

And various anonymous collections appeared with titles such as *A Choice Collection of Riddles, Charades, Rebusses* (1792), *Thesaurus Ænigmaticus* (1725) and *The Masquerade: a collection of new enigmas, logogriphs, charades, rebusses, queries and transpositions* (1797).

However, perhaps the most significant enigmatographer in England during this period was the satirist, poet and author of *Gulliver's Travels*, Dean Swift (1667–1745). Once again these are all very stylish high-brow literary enigmas and were published in serial form in journals like *The Muses Mercury* and the *Miscellanies* (of Pope, Swift, Arbuthnot and Gay) printed by Faulkner in 1727. The subjects vary considerably, as does their length and metre, but perhaps this riddle on gold serves as well as any to illustrate his right to immortality in the pantheon of the world's greatest riddle-masters:

All-ruling Tyrant of the Earth,
To vilest Slaves I owe my birth.
How is the greatest Monarch blest,
When in my gaudy Liv'ry drest!
No haughty Nymph has Pow'r to run
From me; or my Embraces shun.

Stabbed to the Heart, condemned to Flame,
My Constancy is still the same.
The fav'rite Messenger of *Jove*,
And *Lemnian* God consulting strove,
To make me glorious to the Sight
Of Mortals, and the Gods Delight.
Soon would their Altars Flame expire
If I refus'd to lend them Fire.

Riddling Magazines

Swift was not the only riddler to take advantage of the new technology as manifested in the publication of popular and literary magazines in the eighteenth century. In France the Paris-based *Mercure de France* (first published in 1672) soon established itself as the frontrunner of a flourishing industry in society riddling journals, and published occasional writings from many of the leading literary figures of the day. *Énigmes*, logogriphs and charades would appear regularly in this fortnightly pot-pourri of poetry, news and views, with their solutions being given in the following issue. A frequent contributor in the years up to 1810 (after which time the magazine seems to have deemed such bagatelles too frivolous to grace their pages) was the enigmatographer Lamotte (or Lamothe), an example of whose work from the revolutionary month of 'Brumaire' (October) in Year 9 (1800) I give here:

> Avec un guide impitoyable,
> Je parcours les monts chevelus,
> Où je poursuis un monstre, aux humains redoubtable;
> C'est aux jeunes taillis que je chasse le plus,
> Et souvent j'y vais faire un carnage effroyable
> De ces monstres cruels, sous mes dents, abattus.

(With a ruthless guide, I wander over hairy mountains where I pursue a monster, dreaded by humans. It is in the young brushwood that I hunt the most and often I inflict a frightful carnage on those cruel monsters, slaughtered under my teeth.)

The solution is 'a comb'. Journals devoted to riddling mushroomed all over France in this period, another worthy of consideration being the *Magasin énigmatique*, edited by Duchesne. Meanwhile in England, apart from the pages of *The Muses*

Mercury: Or the Monthly Miscellany edited by John Oldmixon, perhaps the most significant forum for the enigmatic art was the *Universal Magazine of Knowledge and Pleasure*. First published in 1747, this monthly periodical can be seen with some justification as giving perhaps the best representative image of English riddling in the eighteenth century. Contributors would pose riddles to be solved (hopefully, but not always) by the next issue and a veritable stampede would follow in which budding literati would attempt to be the first to guess the answers. Here is an example, together with its solution in verse (as was common), by one 'E.R.' from the October issue of 1747:

> Nor wings, nor feet, unto my share have fell,
> Yet I in swiftness do the best excel.
> Arms I have none, nor weapons do I wear,
> And yet I daily wound the brave and fair.
> My name is odious, both to friends and foes,
> Yet I'm admired by all the Belles and Beaus.
> And when my name's concealed, I've many friends,
> The best man fears me, and his fault amends.
> All wise men hate me, as their common foe,
> Take C from me, I keep you from the snow.
> Old maids caress me, for this world I hate,
> As it hates them, so we receive our fate.
> From these short hints, to tell my name's your task,
> That well performed, I've nothing more to ask.

The answer coming in the form:

> She needs no wings: she makes but too much haste.
> She need no weapons; for she wounds too fast.
> Old maids, and belles, and beaus caress the quean.
> And why? She kills their time, and vents their spleen.
> The brave, the wise, the good, she will defame.
> A cursed fiend! and SCANDAL is her name.

However, as with the *Mercure de France*, though the magazine continued well past the eighteenth century, the practice of including riddles amongst its items did not, and by the time of the publication of the new series in 1814 they had disappeared from its pages for ever.

The Chapbook Enigma

However, though multifarious magazines and journals circulated in urban literary society at this time, such periodicals would rarely find their way across the length and breadth of the country. And in the days before national newspapers (*The Times*, then known as *The Daily Universal Register*, did not appear until 1785), penny post, TV and radio, the chapman – a pedlar of household goods, sundry broadsides and cheap pamphlets – was a commonplace and welcome figure in the small communities that dotted the English countryside. Carrying his wares from village to village, the itinerant chapman was often the only contact that many citizens of the realm had with the goings-on of their own government, let alone the outside world. Amongst his political tracts, news-stories (usually somewhat distorted) and varied amusements to while away the long dark evenings were small collections of riddles. Two very popular examples which survive from the eighteenth century are *A Whetstone for Dull Wits* and *The True Trial of Understanding or Wit Newly Revived*. Each only a few pages long, they contain fifteen and nine riddles respectively, beautifully illustrated with explanatory woodcuts. The riddles, some of which are reproduced in Part 2, are of varying lengths and on subjects of a folk-oriented kind such as the following (from *A Whetstone for Dull Wits*):

> By the help of a guide
> I often divide
> What once in a green forest stood;
> Behold me, tho' I
> Have got but one eye,
> When that is stopt I do the most good.

The answer is given as 'A Hatchet, with which they cleave Wood; till the Eye is stopped with the Haft, it cannot perform business.'

Riddle Ballads

Another phenomenon of the history of enigmatography in the eighteenth century was the tradition of anonymous riddle-ballad composition in Britain. These seem to have taken three basic forms:

(i) a riddling contest in which the loser forfeits his life or a wager;

(ii) one where the prize is someone's hand in marriage; and

(iii) a competition in which the 'clever lass' outwits the menfolk.

An example of the first variety is the well-known ballad of 'King John and the Abbot of Canterbury'. This tale appears in many forms in the literature of the period but the plot is basically the same in all versions. The Abbot of Canterbury has accumulated such wealth and power that King John believes he is plotting treason and puts to him three questions which he must answer or lose his head. The Abbot begs three weeks to solve the riddles, but after consulting the best university brains of the time is none the wiser until he meets up with a shepherd who offers to change places with him. The answer the latter gives to the first riddle 'Tell me to one penny what I am worth' is as follows:

> For thirty pence our Saviour was sold
> Among the false Jews, as I have bin told;
> And twenty-nine is the worthe of thee,
> For I thinke thou art one penny worser than hee.

The shepherd continues to solve the other two riddles in similarly humorous vein, which so amuses the king that he offers to make the shepherd Abbot of Canterbury. However, the king relents when the shepherd refuses on grounds of illiteracy, accepting instead a reward and the release of the Abbot.

Examples of the second kind of riddle can be found in ballads such as 'Proud Lady Margaret' – which appears in Sir Walter Scott's *Minstrelsy* (1803), communicated 'by Mr Hamilton, music-seller, Edinburgh with whose mother it had been a favourite' – and 'Captain Wedderburn's Courtship' (see Part 2, pages 158–61). And the 'clever lass' comes into her own in 'A Noble Riddle wisely Expounded or The Maid's answer to the Knight's Three Questions', though the questions certainly seem to number more than three in most versions. Here are a few from Motherwell's MS:

> O what is whiter than the milk?
> Or what is softer than the silk?
>
> O what is sharper than the thorn?
> O what is louder than the horn?

To which the maid responds:

> . . . snow is whiter than the milk,
> And love is softer than the silk.

> O hunger's sharper than the thorn,
> And thunder's louder than the horn.

Further South: Italy in the Eighteenth Century

Anonymity and pseudonymity were also prevalent in Italian riddling of this period and sometimes the writer would go to great lengths to prevent his true identity being discovered.

One of the finest composers of enigmas of this time was Catone l'Uticense Lucchese (Leone Santucci) whose 142 riddling sonnets entitled *Enimmi* first appeared in 1689, were reprinted many times, and were translated into Latin in 1760. Believed to have been a priest, Santucci had a fine sense of humour and is highly esteemed in the history of Italian riddling – his verses being ranked by some as being even better than Straparola's. The subjects dealt with are all totally 'decent' and vary from the learned to the popular, from books to fungus, but are primarily intended, however, as literary exercises, not for general public consumption.

Giovanna Statira Bottini (an anagram for Giovanni Battista Taroni) was a secular priest who died in 1727 having composed numerous oratorios and a highly popular collection of a hundred enigmatic octaves entitled *Cento nodi*. Bottini's riddles, first published in 1718, were much plagiarized in his day and are largely on folk themes. Passing quickly over the work of Chiariti (1784) and Silvano's hundred sonnets (*Ennimi di Lucio Vittore Silvano*, 1793), we come to the enormous enigmatic outpourings of the Venetian 'Fosildo Mirtunzio'. Each of the five *veglie* that make up his *Veglie autunnali* (1796) consists of a hundred octaves and covers an incredible range of subjects, rarely overlapping.

But perhaps the best collection in Italy from the beginning up to the end of the eighteenth century is, along with the works of Malatesti and Catone, that of the pseudonymous 'Moderno Autore'. *Enimmi di Moderno Autore* was first published in Florence in 1797 and contains 152 very carefully written sonnets with subjects such as household objects, but apart from those on insects there are very few riddles on living things. The author also expanded the scope of riddling metres by adding the ancreontic form to the already-established octave and sonnet.

CHAPTER FIVE
The Last Laugh?

With the coming of the nineteenth century there began a gradual decline in the esteem in which the riddle was held. From being at times the quintessential vehicle of high-society humour and literary drollery, it deteriorated at last into a childish amusement. In the same way that the once-subtle art of emblem-writing had lost its prestige almost completely with the advent of Bunyan's *A Book for Boys and Girls* (1686), so too with the publication of such bagatelles as *Pretty Riddle Book* (1805) and *Guess Again or Easy Enigmas & Puzzles for Little Folks* (c.1824) the skills of the enigmatographer became debased into punning parlour games, simple verses in nursery-rhyme books and jokes in Christmas crackers.

It is perhaps symptomatic too that this was the period of the great folklore collectors – Wossidlo, Rolland, Friedreich and, more recently, Archer Taylor – who had begun the painstaking task of clearing up after the cryptic carnival, codifying and pigeon-holing with a dexterity that typified an age when genius was regarded, in Jane Ellice Hopkins's immortal phrase, as being 'an infinite capacity for detail'.

However, this is not to say that top-class riddling had entirely died out and many society figures produced occasional pleasantries to while away the winter evenings, particular interest being aroused by word-puzzles, especially logographs and charades. The celebrated German scientist G. T. Fechner wrote a number of enigmas under the pseudonym 'Dr Mises', and *Neue Räthsel* (1879), by his equally famous compatriot Franz Brentano, was held by Freud to be one of the best modern collections of riddles. Edgar Allan Poe was an accomplished enigmatographer (see Part 2, pages 152–3) and major composers like Elgar, Puccini and Sullivan all adapted their musical talents to include the riddle form at this time. William Whewell also wrote riddles and the great historian Thomas Babington Macaulay is credited with penning the following charade:

> Cut off my head, how singular I act!
> Cut off my tail, and plural I appear!
> Cut off my head and tail – most curious fact!
> Although my middle's left, there's nothing there!
> What is my head, cut off? A sounding sea!
> What is my tail, cut off? A flowing river!
> Amid their mingling depth, I fearless play,
> Parent of softest sounds, though mute forever.

The solution is 'cod'. But somehow the excitement had gone from the art and even the ribald riddle had begun to lose its charm, though bawdy collections such as the *Royal Riddle Book* still appeared (1820). A clear indication of the decline of enigmatography can be seen in the description of Emma Woodhouse's efforts to educate her rather silly pupil Harriet Smith in Jane Austen's *Emma*:

> . . . the only literary pursuit which engaged Harriet at present, the only mental provision she was making for the evening of life, was the collection and transcribing of all the riddles of every sort that she could meet with, into a thin quarto of hot-pressed paper, made up by her friend, and ornamented with cyphers and trophies.

Her efforts were mostly confined to charades like the following (on courtship):

> My first displays the wealth and pomp of kings,
> Lords of the earth! their luxury and ease.
> Another view of man, my second brings,
> Behold him there, the monarch of the seas!
>
> But ah! united what reverse we have!
> Man's boasted power and freedom, all are flown:
> Lord of the earth and sea, he bends a slave,
> And woman, lovely woman, reigns alone.
>
> Thy ready wit the word will soon supply,
> May its approval beam in that soft eye!

Riddle-Rhymes of the Nursery

However, although riddling as a serious entertainment generally died out in nineteenth-century Europe, it nevertheless continued to flourish in a form more adapted to the whims of the childish prankster and survives in this guise even today. From the 'Mother Goose' treasury to the fiendish Gollum of Tolkien's *The Hobbit* there can be no doubt that the telling and invention of riddles plays a very important part in the psychological development of the modern child.

Although strictly speaking a work of the eighteenth century, Robert Samber's translation of Charles Perrault's *Contes de ma mere l'Oye* (1697), which first appeared in John Newbery's edition as *Mother Goose's Tales* (*c*.1729), was a favourite amongst Victorian children and, as well as such well-known fairy stories as *Cinderella* and *The Sleeping Beauty*, it also contained a number of riddles. Typical of the rhyming sing-song style of this collection is the following:

> Black I am and much admired,
> Men seek me until they're tired;
> When they find me, break my head,
> And take me from my resting bed.

to which the solution is 'coal'. The themes tend to centre on everyday objects, animals, heavenly bodies, etc., and they are of varying lengths. Most of them can be found in similar form in general collections of folk riddles from across the globe, as is common with these kinds of enigma.

In a similar vein a good collection of Scottish nursery-rhymes and riddles was made by the publisher Robert Chambers in 1870. Entitled *Popular Rhymes of Scotland*, some of the examples are actually rather fine, such as this one on a cock:

> There was a prophet on this earth,
> His age no man could tell;
> He was at his greatest height
> Before e'er Adam fell.
> His wives are very numerous,
> Yet he maintaineth none;
> And at the day of reckoning
> He bids them all begone.
> He wears his boots when he should sleep;
> His spurs are ever new;
> There's no a shoemaker on a' the earth
> Can fit him for a shoe.

Riddles also appeared in diverse books published specifically with the modern child in mind, such as *The Boy's Own Book* (1829) and its companion volume *The Girl's Own Book* (1832). And such was the popularity of the enigma amongst children of school age that books entirely devoted to the subject began to grace booksellers' shelves, with titles such as *Pretty Riddle Book* by Christopher Conundrum (1805), *Guess Again or Easy Enigmas & Puzzles for Little Folks* (*c*.1824) and a number of penny and halfpenny chapbooks such as *Peter Primrose's Books for Boys and Girls: Riddles* and *The Guess Book* (*c*.1820), from which the following is taken:

> The beginning of eternity,
> The end of time and space,
> The beginning of every end,
> And the end of every place.

The answer is 'the letter E'.

A number of Victorian writers perhaps better known for their adult literary works also took time off to compose enigmas for the playroom, notable amongst these being D. G. Rossetti's sister Christina. Here is an example of hers on pins and needles:

> There is one that has a head without an eye,
>   And there's one that has an eye without a head.
> You may find the answer if you try;
>   And when all is said,
>   Half the answer hangs upon a thread.

As 'Lewis Carroll', the Reverend C. L. Dodgson also wrote a number of books for children, perhaps the most famous of which are the Alice books. In Chapter IX of *Through the Looking Glass* the White Queen tells the following riddle whose answer is not given in the story, but we know from the English periodical *Fun* for 30 October 1878, where a similarly rhyming answer was published by an anonymous author, that it is 'oyster':

> 'First the fish must be caught.'
> That is easy: a baby, I think, could have caught it.
> 'Next, the fish must be bought.'
> That is easy: a penny, I think, would have bought it.
>
> 'Now cook me the fish!'
> That is easy, and will not take more than a minute.
> 'Let it lie in a dish!'

That is easy, because it is already in it.

'Bring it here! Let me sup!'
It is easy to set such a dish on the table.
'Take the dish-cover up!'
Ah, *that* is so hard that I fear I'm unable!

For it holds it like glue –
Holds the lid to the dish, while it lies in the middle:
Which is easiest to do,
Un-dish-cover the fish, or dishcover the riddle?

A very famous conundrum also occurs in Chapter VII, 'A Mad Tea-party', of *Alice's Adventures in Wonderland* where the Mad Hatter asks, 'Why is a raven like a writing desk?' This caused an enormous amount of speculation at the time and though apparently not meant to be taken seriously, Carroll did eventually publish an answer years later: 'Because it can produce a few notes, tho' they are *very* flat; and it is never put with the wrong end in front.' However, other good solutions proposed by the American puzzle genius Sam Loyd are: 'Because Poe wrote on both' and 'Bills and tales are among their characteristics.' Carroll also wrote a number of charades such as the following on a tablet – the first-ever riddle he composed.

A monument – men all agree –
Am I in all sincerity,
    Half cat, half hindrance made.
If head and tail removed should be,
Then most of all you strengthen me;
Replace my head, the stand you see
    On which my tail is laid.

And he would often tease his little girl friends with rebuses like the one depicted opposite taken from a letter written from his sister's house 'The Chestnuts'.

The art of writing books for children which also seem to attract a more adult readership is admirably exemplified in our own time by the works of the late Professor J. R. R. Tolkien. In *The Hobbit* (1937) young Bilbo Baggins is confronted in Chapter 5 by the odious slimy creature Gollum who has lost his magic ring in the labyrinths within the Misty Mountains. A riddle contest ensues, with the object of continuing until one or the other is unable to solve a riddle in three guesses. If Bilbo wins he is to be allowed to

The ●●●● *(snowballs)*

My 🦌 Ina,

    Though 👁 don't give birthday presents, still 👁

April
. . . write a birthday ✉.

June
🦌 came 2 your 🚪 2 wish U many happy returns of the day, 🛢 the 🐱 met me, ✋ took me for a 🐁,

✋ hunted me 👉 and 👉 till 👣 could hardly ⛲. However somehow 👁 got into the 🏠, ✋ there a 🐍 met me, ✋ took me for a 🐿, and pelted me

go free; if not Gollum will eat him. Not surprisingly, after nine genuine riddles such as Gollum's

> This thing all things devours:
> Birds, beasts, trees, flowers;
> Gnaws iron, bites steel;
> Grinds hard stones to meal;
> Slays king, ruins town,
> And beats high mountain down.

to which the answer is 'time', Bilbo decides to cheat a bit and asks, 'What do I have in my pocket?' Gollum suggests 'Handses', knife, and 'String or nothing'. The object is in fact Gollum's ring which Bilbo has found and now slips on to make himself invisible, because though he knew that 'the riddle-game was sacred and of immense antiquity, and even wicked creatures were afraid to cheat when they played at it . . . he felt he could not trust this slimy thing to keep any promise at a pinch'. He guesses correctly and eventually makes good his escape. (The ring, incidentally, is later the salvation of Baggins and his little troop of 'dwarves' and is the mainspring of the plot of the enormously popular sequel *The Lord of the Rings*.)

The modern tradition in children's riddling books continues up to the present day with the publication of such excellent little collections as Ennis Rees's *Riddles, Riddles Everywhere* (1964) and John Cunliffe's *Riddles, Rhymes and Rigmaroles* (1971), both of which are delightfully illustrated. A recent addition is Kit Williams's intriguing picture-book *Masquerade* (1979). Only thirty-two pages long, this charming tale contains in all eight riddles of varying lengths, the solution to each being given in a full-page cryptic illustration facing the text. One such example is a traditional folk riddle to which the answer is 'a hare':

> A hopper o' ditches,
> A cropper o' corn,
> A wee brown cow,
> And a pair of leather horns!

However, the phenomenal commercial success of this slim volume may also be at least partly due to the fact that the solution to all of the riddles provides clues as to the whereabouts of a finely worked piece of jewellery in the form of a golden hare, valued at

£5,000, which the author buried in an undisclosed location before publication. (The hare has now been discovered, however.)

The New Magazines

The same tale of decadence that can be traced in the publication of books of riddles can also be seen to unfold in the history of the riddle as it is found in magazines and journals of the modern period. To be fair, a number of enigmas did appear at intervals in *Notes and Queries* for the year 1865, variously entitled 'Yorkshire Household Riddles' and 'Lincolnshire Household Riddles', but these were merely folk riddles that had been collected by readers. *Punch* has also published a number of conundrums in its pages from time to time, either under the rubric 'Whys and whens, by an eminent professor' (usually eight at a time), or at the bottoms of columns as fillers, a particularly good illustrated example from an issue of 1843 being:

Why is a solar eclipse like a mother thrashing her own child? –
Because it's a hiding of the sun.

(The picture shows a rather recalcitrant child being set about with a stick by a hard-faced old matron wearing a mob cap.)

However, although *The Riddle Magazine: a journal of poetry, puzzles, and pastimes* was published in 1873 and an Italian monthly periodical, *Ennimistica moderno*, devoted exclusively to riddles, appeared in Turin in 1924, today's riddler-in-the-street is hard put to find any regular serious publication to cater for his whims, as most modern quiz magazines deal largely with acrostics and crossword puzzles. It is true that a very popular series of rebuses did feature in the newspaper columns of Sam Loyd in the United States at the turn of the century, but perhaps the most widely read examples of magazine enigmas available in modern times are those that appear in children's comics – the antics of such arch-fiends as the enigmatic villain known as 'the Riddler', who terrorizes the Gotham City of the American D.C. Comics' Batman series, being a case in point. Today's youngsters are well acquainted with his cryptic clues to the 'Dynamic Duo' concerning the whereabouts of his next crime – an example being the scrap of paper which Batman finds in the episode entitled 'Riddles in the Dark' (August 1980 issue), on which is written 'When is a horse most like a stamp collection?' The answer is 'When it's a hobby horse', which indicates that the Riddler is at Hobby Airport, Houston.

Contemporary Riddling in the Third World and Elsewhere

In spite of its apparent decline in the West, riddling is still practised by adults in many countries of the Third World, from the Indians of the Americas to African tribesmen, and from the villagers of Asia to the peasantry of rural Russia. Serious contests and riddle rituals can still be seen taking place amongst Yoruba, Afrikaners and Parsees, and adult games involving the telling of enigmas continue to be popular throughout the Third World.

In South Africa the oral tradition survives amongst the Hottentots, and Bushmen puzzle over enigmas involving all kinds of animals and hunting, whilst the Bantu have a very wide-ranging collection with examples like the following: 'What shows no mark when it is hit?', to which the answer is 'water'. According to Sir James Frazer in *The Golden Bough* (written at the turn of the century), the rain-making ceremonies of one particular African tribe involve naked women dancing and shouting, and if any men are found in the neighbourhood whilst this is going on they are beaten and quizzed with obscene riddles alluding to their circumcision rituals.

Riddles of the English-speaking inhabitants of the country tend to reflect those disseminated in Europe and so do not concern us here, but amongst the Afrikaners a great many original riddles have been found and over 2,000 were published in 1954 in G. A. van Rooyen and S. H. Pellisier's book *Raai, raai, riepa, of Die Afrikaanse raaiselbok*. Many of them rhyme like the following:

It is coloured and round.
It has a pot belly,
It lies on the ground,
It blows at a fellow.
A dog it kisses
And kills while it hisses.

to which the answer is 'a puff-adder'.

The Yoruba of Nigeria also have a large store of enigmas, though many are based on knowledge of their particular institutions and are hence difficult for an outsider to appreciate. One example of a more general nature is this riddle on a drum:

> They cut off his head; they cut off his waist; his stump says he will call the town together.

The Kxatla enjoy riddle contests with subjects such as fingers: 'Ten boys with their hats on the back of their heads'; or bread: 'The white horse goes into the stable and comes out brown'. The Nyanja have 'The hide in the middle, the meat outside' as a riddle for the gizzard, and the Tlokwa signify snowing in the description 'The white goats are descending from the mountain'.

The Parsees of India also have a long-established tradition of riddling that continues today. For example: 'Coat after coat do I put on and hot-tempered am I' is an onion, and a lighted lamp is described as a 'golden parrot drinking water with its tail.' A Latin-American riddle on a bell runs:

> A lazy old woman
> has a tooth in her crown,
> and with that tooth
> she gathers the people.

whilst a collection of Macedonian folklore provides us with the following on a chestnut:

> Without as smooth as glass,
> Within a woolly mass.
> But hid amid the wool
> There lurks a nice mouthful.

The End of the Enigma?

Exactly *why* riddling in modern, highly industrialized societies seems to have deteriorated from being an adult literary entertainment into a pastime for children, yet continues undaunted in rural communities of the Third World and elsewhere, is an enigma in itself. Has it something to do with the different cultural backgrounds of the civilizations involved, the dependence or alienation created by the presence/absence of increased technology, or just varying temperaments? Is riddling something only relevant to cultures at the so-called 'mythological' stage of thought or has all the fun gone out of the Western world?

Sir James Frazer racked his brains over this issue nearly a hundred years ago to no avail and it is certainly beyond the scope of this book to investigate the matter further. However, recent research by a number of eminent psychologists, sociologists and anthropologists, together with the novel light shed on our thinking processes by the work of writers such as Edward de Bono, and new insights into play behaviour by Johann Huizinga *(Homo Ludens)* and Opie and Opie *(The Lore and Language of Schoolchildren)* have begun to make some inroads into this shady area of our knowledge.

One interesting insight that *has* emerged from these early exploratory attempts is that, in the West at least, interest in riddles seems to coincide with seasons of intellectual awakening – something that has certainly been borne out by the researches for the present anthology. Whether during the classic period of Greek culture, early Anglo-Saxon Britain, the flowering of the Middle Ages and Renaissance in Europe, or the stately grandeur of court life in the seventeenth and eighteenth centuries, the riddle has always appeared hand in hand with a resurgence in artistic activity, almost as a touchstone of cultural finesse. And who knows? With the advent of executive toys, 'Space Invaders' in pubs, high-brow lectures on Tolkien and Lewis Carroll, international crossword (and even tiddlywink) competitions, not to mention *Masquerade*, the maddeningly successful 'Cube' and the increased audiences for cryptic quiz programmes and 'whodunnits' (many of which are currently being filmed), could it be that the play instinct, and specifically a delight in mystery games and puzzling, really is returning to our microchip-manacled society? Or will that great riddle-master, Time, have the very last laugh?

PART TWO

A Worldwide Riddle Anthology

Author's Note

This section of the book is intended primarily as an anthology of nearly 1,000 riddles selected from the enormous literature on the subject, with the aim of trying to give a representative cross-section of the material currently available. Some riddles, especially those in Latin, French and Italian, appear here in translation for the first time, though no attempt has been made to imitate the (usually exquisite) verse forms of the originals. The riddles are generally arranged alphabetically by author, except in cases where the authorship is not known, when the entries can be found under the title of the work in question. Solutions for all the riddles can be found on pages 195–205.

ADEVINEAUX AMOUREUX, Les (1478)
Anonymous French riddle collection printed in Bruges.

1. Between two legs the living flesh ambles,
   Between two buttocks the living flesh trembles,
   And when it comes to the door,
   Its master knocks.

2. Two who run and ten who chase them, two who look on, and one who puts them to death.

ALDHELM of Malmesbury, St (d. 709)
Bishop of Sherborne and Abbot of Malmesbury. Riddles contained in *Epistola ad Acircium*.

3. Long since, the holy power that made all things
   So made me that my master's dangerous foes
   I scatter. Bearing weapons in my jaws,
   I soon decide fierce combats; yet I flee
   Before the lashings of a little child.

4. Now does my wondrous life attract the mind.
   I, clothed in scales, with schools of fish explore
   The reaches of the sea, or with the birds
   Mount through the upper air on soaring wings,
   And yet I can not live by breathing air.

5. Once I was water, full of scaly fish;
   But, by a new decision, Fate has changed
   My nature: having suffered fiery pangs,
   I now gleam white, like ashes or bright snow.

6. Cold from the earth's chill bowels was I brought.
   My foursquare head will smooth down hardest iron;
   And I shall never fear vicissitudes
   Of age, so long as Mulciber by fire
   Snatch not away the number of my years:
   Grim heat soon softens my unyielding form.

7. Incongruous is my visage to my frame:
   Though horns are on my head, the rest of me
   Appears a hideous man; by fame well known
   Through all the Gnossian land, a bastard, born
   In Crete of unknown sire, by double name
   Of man and beast together I am called.

8. Both shining white am I and dusky black
   Together, decked with parti-coloured plumes.
   No trilling voice is mine, for with my beak
   I utter ugly sounds. Though scaly snakes
   I catch and rend – to them a fearsome foe –
   Death-dealing venom never swells my veins;
   Nay more, I even feed my fluffy chicks
   With poisoned flesh and loathful serpents' blood.

9. The dewy earth's cold vitals gave me birth;
   I am not made of rough wool, and no loom
   Has ever stretched me, nor its humming thread
   Leapt back and forth, nor have the Chinese worms
   Woven me of their saffron floss. By wheels
   I was not tortured, nor by carding combs.
   Yet, lo, the people christen me 'a coat'.
   No arrow in the quiver frightens me.

10. Though dainty is my shape, keen spurs I wear;
    In swarms I wing my way above the peaks.
    I get red booty with my reeking blade,
    And spare no four-legged beast, but its coarse flesh

With goading darts I wound; once fame I won,
Vexing the land of Memphis. Now I pierce
The swelling brawn of bulls, and taste their blood.

11. My four feet tread the surface of the waves,
Yet not a fear have I of falling in,
But walk on land and water equally.
Nature forbids me swim the rushing stream,
Or boisterous rivers cross by bridge or boat;
Rather, I glide dry-foot upon the flood.

12. My heavy body and great limbs sprout plumes;
I have the falcon's hue, but not his flight,
For through the upper air my scanty wings
Could never bear me; rather, I must pace
On foot through dirty fields. Smooth eggs I lay,
To make men cups. Phoenician Africa,
So runs the rumour, is my native land.

13. I haunt, all pale, the waters of foul fens;
Fortune has fashioned me a bloody name,
For greedy gulps of red blood are my fare.
No bones, or feet, or arms at all have I,
Yet bite with three-forked wounds unlucky men,
And by health-bringing lips thus conquer care.

14. Of cold and hardness did my sire and dam
Beget me, but I speedily grew strong
Upon dry tinder; nourished by such food,
I now can conquer fortune, for no thing
But water ever can subdue my power.
The wooded uplands, rocks – yea, iron and tin –
I menace, when I loose my natural force.
While life is warm in me, no star of heaven
Outshines me; when at last my race is run,
The blackest pitch is not so black as I.

15. The Greek and Latin tongues both named me thus:
The thousand-leaf, that springs from verdant turf;
My name thus holds ten hundred in its span.
My stalk bears leaves as does no other plant's
In all the unnumbered furrows of the earth.

16. Born of my own free will, on fertile sod
I flourish. Yellow flowers adorn my head.
At morn I open, close at setting sun,
And hence the clever Greeks devised my name.

17. Of two materials have open palms
    Moulded me. Gleaming white am I within –
    My vitals are the shining spoil of flax,
    Or slender rush; but all my outer parts
    Are yellow with a colour born of flowers;
    They vomit forth hot, fiery flames, and melt,
    Dripping a rain of tear-drops from my brows;
    Thus I dispel the fearful shades of night.
    My vitals burn, and naught but ashes leave.

18. Upon steep banks along the stream I dwell –
    Not slothful, but by weapons of my mouth
    Made warlike – and endure a life of toil,
    With hook-shaped axes felling heavy trees.
    Down to the oozy bottom, where the fish
    Swim to and fro, I often plunge, and drench
    My head in many an eddy. I can cure
    Ills of the bowels, heal corrupted limbs,
    Dispel the pestilence and deadly plague.
    For food I gnaw the bitter bark of trees.

19. The shining pelican, whose yawning throat
    Gulps down the waters of the sea, long since
    Produced me, white as he. Through snowy fields
    I keep a straight road, leaving deep-blue tracks
    Upon the gleaming way, and darkening
    The fair champaign with black and tortuous paths;
    Yet one way through the plain suffices not,
    For with a thousand bypaths runs the road,
    And them who stray not from it, leads to heaven.

20. First, from earth's bosom was I brought, and shaped
    Artfully, while the rest of me was made
    From a ferocious bull or fetid goat.
    Through me the eyes of many close in death –
    Through me, who, bare of armour, yet essay
    To guard my master's life; my house is built
    Of shapen hide and smooth wood split from trees.

21. In dewy drops I come from rainy skies,
    And swell in form by falling with the shower.
    No hand may touch me as I float along
    Among the eddies, for a single touch
    Instantly bursts me, and my fragile breath
    Into thin air departs. But now I swim,
    And lead whole cohorts in my company,
    Since many comrades share my origin.

22. When God by flood was punishing vile sin,
    And by those waters cleansing evil's stain,
    I first fulfilled the patriarch's command,
    As by a fruitful bough I signified
    Salvation to the earth was come. Thenceforth
    My heart is ever gentle, and in me,
    A happy bird, no black bile ever flows.

23. I am the faithful guardian of the house,
    And vigilantly keep it all night long,
    Roaming among blind shadows, for my eyes
    Lose not their light, though in a pitchy cave.
    In crafty ambush for such cursed thieves
    As prey upon the stored-up grain, I set
    The silent snares of death, and prying, find
    The lair of beasts, a roving huntress I.
    Yet will I not pursue the fleeing bands
    With baying hounds, for dogs would turn on me,
    And bark at me their threat of cruel war.
    A race I hate has given me my name.

24. The Lord Creator both of feet and hands
    Defrauded me, when first he set in place
    The world immeasurable. I do not fly,
    Borne on the pinions of a bird; no breath
    Livens my body with recurrent gusts.
    I may behold the vaulted arch of heaven,
    Yet scorn not rolling ocean's broad expanse.

25. In sluggish stream I flowed from rifted rocks,
    As flames broke up the stones, and fire applied
    The unleashed ardour of the furnace-heat;
    My form capacious now is clear as ice.
    Yea, many long to hold me in their hand,
    Fingering my slippery shape in dainty grasp;
    But I befool their minds, the while I lay
    Sweet kisses on their lips that press me close,
    And urge their tottering footsteps to a fall.

26. Now in one body I have twice six eyes
    And twice three heads, but all my other parts
    Rule these. Upborne on twice two feet I walk,
    And yet my body's nails are ninety-six.
    In number like a metric syzygy
    I thus appear. The poplar and the yew
    And green-leaved willow-tree I hate, but love
    The crooked beech-tree with its nuts, and oaks

With thick-crowned head that juicy acorns bear,
Nor do I scorn the holm-oak with its shade.

27. Now I shall tell what you can scarce believe,
    Though true it is, not foolish trickery:
    For once I gave my son a pleasing gift,
    A gift which none could ever give to me,
    Since God on high withheld this glorious boon,
    In which all other men rejoice their hearts.

28. Of all that breathe refreshing air of heaven,
    I am most cunning, who through all the world
    Flung wide the seeds of death, whence sprang a crop
    Of grim and hideous grain; there with his scythe,
    Measuring the yield to serve his evil plans,
    Roams the Defiler. Never dare I fight
    The stag with branching antlers. When old age
    Falls on me, I cast off my worn-out skin,
    And find my body staunch, my youth renewed.

29. Six eyes are mine; as many ears have I;
    Fingers and toes twice thirty do I bear.
    Of these, when forty from my flesh are torn,
    Lo, then but twenty will remain to me.

30. What earthly thing is armed with might like mine,
    Or boldly strives to use such force and strength?
    Small was my life's beginning, but great things,
    Though I am slender, low I lay in death,
    A death my belly's inmost hollow hides.
    For woodlands dense, groves, shrubs, and mountains tall,
    Pine forests on their flanks, I murderously –
    Savage and greedy, with capacious maw –
    Lay waste, and scatter wide beneath the sky;
    And yet my form was slighter than a gnat's
    When first my icy mother brought me forth,
    Producing offspring from her stony womb.

ALEXIS (*c.* 375–*c.* 275 BC)

Ancient Greek poet and dramatist. Riddle cited in Athenaeus's *Deipnosophistae*.

31. It is not mortal nor yet immortal; rather, it has a nature so mixed
    that its life is neither in man's estate nor in a god's, but its substance
    ever grows fresh and then dies again; it may not be seen by the eye,
    yet it is known of all.

AL-HARIRI, Abu Muhammad Al-Qasim (1054–1122)

Arab grammarian and intelligence officer from Basra, Iraq. Riddles contained in *Maqamat* ('Assemblies').

32. Rise, my dear son, may thy luck not set, nor thy adversary keep on foot, take with thee the one of full-moon face and of pearly hue, of pure root and tormented body, who was pinched and stretched, imprisoned and released, made to drink and weaned, and pushed into the fire, after he had been slapped. Then career to the market the career of the longing swain, and bring back instead of it the pregnant that impregnates, the spoiler who enriches, the saddener who gladdens, the possessor of a puff that sets on fire, and of a germ that breaks forth in light, of an emission [utterance] that satisfies, and of a gift that profits, who, when he is struck, thunders and lightens, and reveals himself in flames, and who sputters on tinder-rags.

33. A maiden I know, brisk, full of speed in her ministry, returning the same track that she went by when starting off:

   A driver she has, kinsman of hers, who is urging her, but while he thus is speeding her on, is her helpmate too.

   In summer she is seen dew-besprinkled and moist and fresh, when summer is gone, her body shows flabby and loose and dry.

34. A son there is of a mother fair, whose root has sprung from her lofty plant:

   He hugs her neck, though for some time, she had erewhile discarded him:

   He who reaps her beauty ascends by means of him and none forbids and blames.

35. One split in his head it is through whom 'the writ' is known, as honoured recording angels take their pride in him;

   When given to drink he craves for more, as though athirst, and settles to rest when thirstiness takes hold of him;

   And scatters tears about him when ye bid him run, but tears that sparkle with the brightness of a smile.

36. One restless, although firmly fixed, bestowing gifts, not working mischief,

   Now plunging, now uprising again, a marvel how he sinks and soars:

   He pours down tears as one oppressed, yet is his fierceness to be feared:

   For then he brings destruction on, although his inmost heart is pure.

37. One of whose sharpness I fight shy, he grows without either food,
    or drink. . . .

38.   What is the thing, that when it corrupts, its error turns to
    righteousness,
        And when its qualities are choice it stirs up mischief where it
    appears:
        Its parent is of pure descent, but wicked that which he begets.

39. And people who in their flight in eagle's wake sped along, although
    they were heavily arrayed in helmet and steel.

40. And oftentimes passed me by a dog in whose mouth there was a
    bull, but know ye, it was a bull without any tail.

AMUSING RIDDLE BOOK, The (1830)

41. My habitation's in a wood,
    And I'm at any one's command.
    I often do more harm than good:
    If once I get the upper hand,
    I never fear a champion's frown;
    Stout things I often times have done;
    Brave soldiers I can fell them down,
    I never fear their sword nor gun.

ANONYMOUS
A selection of riddles, mostly of folk origin, drawn from a wide variety
of sources including Wossidlo's *Mecklenburgische Volksüberlieferungen*
(1897), Chambers's *Popular Rhymes of Scotland* (1870) and Taylor's
Riddles from Oral Tradition (1951).

42. Riddlum, riddlum, raddy,
    All head and no body.

43. Them has got eyes ain't got no head,
    An' what got head ain't got eyes.

44. What has a face,
    But no mouth?

45. What has a neck but no head?

46. A riddle, a riddle, as I suppose;
    A hundred eyes and never a nose.

47. What has a tongue but no mouth?

48. East and west and north and south,
    One hundred teeth and never a mouth.

49. As I was going over London Bridge, I saw something in the hedge. It had four fingers and one thumb, and was neither fish, flesh, fowl nor bone.

50. What has feet and legs and nothing else?

51. Sometimes with a head,
Sometimes with no head at all,
Sometimes with a tail,
Sometimes with no tail at all.
What am I?

52. It stands on its one leg with its heart in its head.

53. What is this?
Only two backbones,
A thousand ribs.

54. What is it has four legs, one head and a foot?

55. Long legs, crooked toes,
Glassy eyes, snotty nose.

56. Riddle me, riddle me, riddle me ree,
I saw a nut cracker up in a tree.

57. There was a thing just four weeks old,
When Adam was no more;
Before that thing was five weeks old.
Old Adam was fourscore.

58. Something was here since the world was first made, and just a month old. What's that?

59. Cut me up in pieces and bury me alive,
The young ones will live and the old ones die.

60. I never was, am always to be,
None ever saw me, nor ever will,
And yet I am the confidence of all
Who live and breathe on this terrestrial ball.

61. When first I appear I seem mysterious,
But when I am explained I am nothing serious.

62. I am taken from a mine, and shut up in a wooden case, from which I am never released, and yet I am used by almost everybody.

63. What runs all day and all night and never stops?

64. What is it that goes uphill and downhill yet never moves?

65. What turns without moving?

66. What goes out but never comes back?

67. What goes up and never comes down?

68. What is it that goes to the water, and the first that touches the water is the arse?

69. What goes through the woods and never touches a thing?

70. What goes round the house and in the house and never touches the house?

71. Over the water and under the water and never touches the water.

72. What goes away above the ground
    And returns under it?

73. What goes over the water and under the water,
    And never touches the water?

74. What can pass before the sun without making a shadow?

75. What walks all day on its head?

76. What goes to the wood facing home?

77. What goes round and round the wood and never gets into the wood?

78. What is it goes from house to house and never goes in?

79. Goes to the door and doesn't knock,
    Goes to the window and doesn't rap,
    Goes to the fire and doesn't warm,
    Goes upstairs and does no harm.

80. Runs smoother than any rhyme,
    Loves to fall but cannot climb.

81. What makes a lot of noise
    In a house with one door,
    And if it sits in a draft,
    You can't hear it no more?

82. Never sings a melody, never has a song,
    But it goes on humming all day long.

83. If you feed it it will live,
    If you give it water it will die.

84. I'm in everyone's way,
    Yet no one I stop;
    My four arms in every way play,
    And my head is nailed on at the top.

85. What has a head but cannot think?

86. What kind of ear cannot hear?

87. What has a mouth but cannot talk?

88. What has a bed but never sleeps; and has a mouth, yet never eats?

89. What is it that has a tongue but never talks,
Has no legs but always walks?

90. What has teeth but cannot eat?

91. What has four legs and one back but can't walk?

92. What has got eyes but never sees?
What has got a tongue but never talks?
What has a soul that can't be saved?

93. What has four eyes and cannot see?

94. What has a thousand legs and can't walk?

95. What is it which flies high and flies low, has no feet and yet wears shoes?

96. A white dove flew down by the castle. Along came a king and picked it up handless, ate it up toothless, and carried it away wingless.

97. I have a cock on yonder hill,
I keep him for a wonder,
And every time the cock do crow,
It lightens, hails and thunders.

98. A hopper o' ditches,
A cropper o'corn,
A wee brown cow,
And a pair of leather horns!

99. A cow calved it; it grew in the woods; and a smith made it.

100. We have a horse
Without any head;
He is never alive,
And never will be dead.

101. A steel horse going over a bony bridge with a silver whip to drive him.

102. Without a Bridle,
Or a Saddle,
Across a thing.
I Ride a-straddle.
And those I Ride,
By help of me,
Tho' almost Blind,
Are made to see.

103. Goes over the fields all day,
Sits in the cupboard at night.

104. What goes all down the street and comes back home, and sits in the corner and waits for a bone with its tongue hanging out?

105. Runs over fields and woods all day.
Under the bed at night sits not alone,
With long tongue hanging out
A–waiting for a bone.

106. Two legs sat upon three–legs,
One–leg knocked two–legs off three–legs,
Two–legs hit four–legs with three–legs.

107. At night they come without being fetched, and by day they are lost without being stolen.

108. The calf, the goose and the bee,
The world is ruled by these three.

109. My back and belly is wood,
And my ribs is lined with leather.
I've a hole in my nose and one in my breast,
And I'm oftenest used in cold weather.

110. Little Polly Pickett
Run through the thicket,
Out and in and back again
With one leg tied to the door jamb.

111. Long neck and no hands,
Hundred legs and can't stand,
Runs through the house of a morning,
Stands behind the door when company comes.

112. Long–legged lifeless came to the door staffless,
More afraid of a rooster and hen
Than he was of a dog and ten men.

113. No mouth, no eyes,
Nor yet a nose,
Two arms, two feet,
And as it goes,
The feet don't touch the ground,
But all the way,
The head runs round.

114. There was a prophet on this earth,
His age no man could tell;
He was at his greatest height

Before e'er Adam fell.
His wives are very numerous,
Yet he maintaineth none;
And at the day of reckoning
He bids them all begone.
He wears his boots when he should sleep;
His spurs are ever new;
There's no a shoemaker on a' the earth
Can fit him for a shoe.

115. A little informer,
Clothed in bright armour,
Beloved by men of degree;
It goes fine and neat,
Without leg or feet,
Now tell me what this riddle must be.

116. It was neither fish, flesh, nor bone,
And they said it had horns and wasn't a beast.

117. Little Jessie Ruddle, sitting in a puddle, green garters and yellow
toes. Tell me this riddle or I'll smash your nose!

118. Fatherless and motherless,
Born without a skin,
Spoke when it came into the world
And never spoke again.

119. Why is a baby like a wheatfield?

120. They took me from my mother's side
Where I was bravely bred
And when to age I did become
They did cut off my head.
They gave to me some diet drink
That often made me mad
But it made peace between two kings
And made two lovers glad.

121. I sailed here from the old land,
And am bound with iron bonds;
Murder have I not done;
Stolen not; cheated not;
Yet a peg is beaten into my head.

122. What force or strength cannot get through,
I, with gentle touch, can do;
And many in the street could stand,
Were I not, as a friend, at hand.

123. What is it that, after we have fastened, bolted, locked, barred the house, placed a watchman on guard, and taken the keys with us, yet before morning, goes out in spite of us?

124. I tremble at each breath of air,
And yet can heaviest burdens bear.

125. No principal or teacher, I can make every one in the world talk without saying a single word.

126. What gets wet when drying?

127. Brass cap and wooden head,
Spits fire and spews lead.

128. What shoemaker makes shoes without leather,
With all four elements put together?
Fire and water, earth and air;
Every customer has two pair.

129. As I went over Padstow Bridge
Upon a cloudy day,
I met a fellow, clothed in yellow,
I took him up and sucked his blood,
And threw his skin away.

130. As I went out one moonlight night,
I saw a thing that made me fright.
I hit it hard and heavy blows
Till it bled gallons at the nose.

131. Use me well and I am everybody;
Scratch my back and I am nobody.

132. I sat on my hunkers,
I looked through my peepers,
I saw the dead burying the living.

133. As I went over London Bridge,
I saw a little house: I looked in
Through the window, and there was
A red man making a black man sing.

134. As I was on my way to London Town
To buy my wife a soda cracker,
I saw a host: some black, some brown,
The rest the colour of tobacker.

135. There was a green house.
Inside the green house there was a white house.
Inside the white house there was a red house.
Inside the red house there were a lot of little black babies.

136. Three men going to heaven: one goes halfway and turns back, one
     goes right up, and one doesn't go at all.

137. Behind the king's kitchen there is a great vat,
     And a great many workmen working at that,
     Yellow is their toes, yellow is their clothes.
     Tell me this riddle and you can pull my nose.

138. Out in the garden
     I have a green spot,
     And twenty-four ladies dancing on that;
     Some in green gowns,
     And some in blue caps.
     You are a good scholar,
     If you riddle me that.

139. Four boys were walking along the street.
     Two were big and two were small,
     And the two in front were walking quick,
     And the two behind were walking quick.
     Although the two in front stop,
     The two behind could not catch them.

140. There were five men walking along and it started to rain.
     The four that ran got wet and the one that stood still stayed dry.

141. There is a thing that when it has a root, it has no leaves; and when
     it pulls up its root, the leaves appear.

142. Yonder stands a tree of honour,
     Twelve limbs grow upon her;
     Every limb a different name,
     It would take a wise man to tell you the same.

143. Lives in winter,
     Dies in summer,
     And grows with its root upwards.

144. The land was white,
     The seed was black.
     It'll take a good scholar
     To riddle me that.

145. I washed my hands with water,
     Which was neither rain nor run,
     I dried them on a towel,
     Which was neither woven nor spun.

146. As I went across the bridge, I met a man with a load of wood
     which was neither straight nor crooked. What kind of wood was it?

147. In marble walls as white as milk,
Lined with a skin as soft as silk;
Within a fountain crystal clear,
A golden apple doth appear.
No doors there are to this stronghold
Yet thieves break in and steal the gold.

148. As I was going to Worcester, I met a man from Gloucester. I asked him where he was going, and he told me to Gloucester to buy something that had neither top nor bottom but which could hold flesh, blood, and bones.

149. What is round as a dishpan, deep as a tub, and still the oceans couldn't fill it up?

150. Patch upon patch without any stitches,
Riddle me that and I'll buy you a pair of breeches.

151. What is that which 20 will go into a tankard, and one will fill a barn?

152. What is black and white and red all over?

153. What belongs to you,
But others use it more than you do?

154. What is it that you can keep after giving it to someone else?

155. What goes to sleep with its shoes on?

156. What goes up the chimney down,
But can't go down the chimney up?

157. Light as a feather,
Nothing in it.
A stout man can't hold it
More than a minute.

158. What is it that you will break even if you name it?

159. What fastens two people yet touches only one?

160. What is it the more you take away the larger it becomes?

161. What grows larger the more you contract it?

162. My first is in south but not in north,
My second is in picture but not in film,
My third is in fourth and also in worth,
My fourth is in book and also in cook,
My fifth is in toe but not in sew,
My sixth is in life but not in death.

163. What comes once in a minute, twice in a moment, but not once in a thousand years?

164. The more you take, the more you leave behind. What are they?

165. My first is in apple and also in pear,
My second is in desperate and also in dare,
My third is in sparrow and also in lark,
My fourth is in cashier and also in clerk.
My fifth is in seven and also in ten,
My whole is a blessing indeed unto men.

166. Hoddy-doddy,
With a round black body!
Three feet and a wooden hat;
What's that?

167. Riddle me, riddle me, what is that
Over the head and under the hat?

168. What God never sees,
What the king seldom sees;
What we see every day:
Read my riddle – I pray.

169. I've seen you where you never was,
    And where you ne'er will be;
And yet you in that very same place
    May still be seen by me.

170. Over the water,
And under the water,
And always with its head down!

171. I saw a fight the other day;
A damsel did begin the fray.
She with her daily friend did meet;
Then standing in the open street,
She gave such hard and sturdy blows,
He bled ten gallons at the nose;
Yet neither seem to faint nor fall,
Nor gave her any abuse at all.

172. There is a bird of great renown,
Useful in city and in town;
None work like unto him can do;
He's yellow, black, red, and green,.
A very pretty bird I mean;
Yet he's both fierce and fell:
I count him wise that can this tell.

173. There is a flying thing, which stays anywhere – even in the forests;
its face is the face of a cow, its neck the neck of a horse, its breast

the breast of a man, its wing is like a leaf in blossom, its tail resembles a snake and its feet look like the feet of a bird.

174. When one does not know what it is, then it is something; but when one knows what it is, then it is nothing.

175. A water lock and a wooden key, the hunter is captured and the game escapes.

176. To ease men of their care
I do both rend and tear
Their mother's bowels still;
Yet though I do,
There are but few
That seem to take it ill.

177. What shows no mark when it is hit?

178. What is it that a mother loves very dearly, but which can never welcome her when she comes home?

179. I saw a wonderful thing. It had four legs but no soul, it gets many thousand thrusts but does not feel them, it has tulips and violets in full bloom, but you cannot hear the sigh of a nightingale.

180. There is a city, people go about in it, but one sees no streets.

181. Who flays himself, does not die from it, and walks without feet?

182. What has four wings and can't fly, no legs but can go?

183. What is as black as a priest, leaps like a horse, and a hundred men can't bridle it?

184. A rooster without trousers with a red moustache runs all over woods and mountains, and when he finds water, he perishes.

185. A hollow ship with freight of slops,
Inside a cave her anchor drops.

186. What is it that a man buys for three pence, boils in a quart of salt, and then salts some more when it has boiled?

187. Not bigger than a grain of barley, and it covers the table of a king.

188. Who is it who has neither bones nor a skeleton, who carries fire on his head?

189. A little rod in Alexander's wood, neither pine is it, nor oak is it, it is no wood on earth, and you will not guess it till nightfall.

190. A hundred-year-old man and his head one night old.

191. A tree which you cut down today and the next it begins to sprout.

192. He comes to you amidst the brine, the butterfly of the sun, the man of coat so blue and fine, with red thread his shirt is done.

193. It has neither mouth, nor teeth, nor bowels;
    Yet it eats its food steadily.
    It has neither village, nor home, nor hands, nor feet;
    Yet it wanders everywhere.
    It has neither country, nor means, nor office, nor pen;
    Yet it is ready for fight always.
    By day and by night there is wailing about it.
    It has no breath; yet to all it appears.

194. White are the walls, green are the men, brown are the priests, who
    sleep in the monastery.

195. What holds water yet is full of holes?

196. What goes into the water red and comes out black?

197. What goes into the water black and comes out red?

198. What goes up and down stairs without moving?

199. Round the rocks
    And round the rocks
    The ragged rascal ran,
    And every bush he came to
    He left his rags and ran.

200. What grows in the woods,
    Winters in the town,
    And earns its master many a crown?

201. As I went over Lincoln Bridge,
    I met Mister Rusticap;
    Pins and needles on his back,
    A-going to Thorny Fair.

202. As round as an apple,
    As deep as a pail;
    It never cries out
    Till it's caught by the tail.

203. The robbers came to our house,
    When we were all in.
    The house lap out at the windows,
    And we were all taken.

204. Behind the bush, behind the thorn,
    I heard a stout man blow his horn,
    He was booted and spurred, and stood with pride,
    With golden feathers at his side;
    His beard was flesh, and his mouth was horn,
    I am sure such a man never could have been born.

205. Arthur Bower has broken his band;
     He comes roaring up the land;
     The King of Scots, with all his power,
     Cannot turn Arthur of the Bower.

206. Formed long ago, yet made today,
     Employed while others sleep;
     What few would like to give away,
     Nor any wish to keep.

207. As black as ink and isn't ink
     As white as milk and isn't milk
     As soft as silk and isn't silk
     And hops about like a filly-foal.

208. Long legs, crooked thighs
     Little head and no eyes.

209. Hitty Pitty within the wall
     Hitty Pitty without the wall
     If you touch Hitty Pitty
     Hitty Pitty will bite you.

210. Crooked as a rainbow,
     Slick as a plate,
     Ten thousand horses
     Can't pull it straight.

211. Humpty Dumpty sat on a wall,
     Humpty Dumpty had a great fall,
     All the king's horses and all the king's men
     Couldn't put Humpty Dumpty together again.

212. The man who made it did not want it;
     The man who bought it did not use it;
     The man who used it did not know it.

213. Brothers and sisters have I none but that man's father is my father's
     son.

214. What is big at the bottom, little at the top, and has ears?

215. What is green on the mountain, black in the market-place, and red
     in the house?

216. What has a head like a cat, feet like a cat, tail like a cat, but is not a
     cat?

217. It's as round's the moon,
     An' as clear's crystal;
     An ye dinna tell ma riddle,
     I'll shoot ye wi' ma pistol!

218. What small chest is full of mouse bones?

219. He who has it doesn't tell it;
     He who takes it doesn't know it;
     He who knows it doesn't want it.

220. It has cities, but no houses;
     It has forests, but no trees;
     It has rivers, but no fish.
     What is it?

221. What is this: there's a sweetshop inside a lumber shop inside a
     leather shop inside a thorn shop?

222. Who spends the day at the window, goes to the table for meals and
     hides at night?

223. Upon a white lake there sits a red rose,
     But he who would speak with the white lake
     Must first break the red rose.

224. In my father's garden stand many trees. Each tree has many
     branches and on each branch hang cradles and in the cradles lie
     children.

225. When I was young and beautiful
     I wore a blue crown.
     When I was old and stiff
     They tied a rope around my body.
     Then I was cudgelled and beaten
     And dragged away from house and home.

226. I have a little house which I live in all alone,
     Without doors, without windows,
     And if I want to go out I have to break through the wall.

227. I am a poor iron knight,
     I have no arms but always point right.
     I have no feet but I must always go
     And must stand on duty both day and night through.
     If ever I rest, all will complain.

228. I carry the heaviest loads and yet I have no back. Men and beasts
     from far and wide tramp over me and I always stay in the same
     place.

229. If I stand still and don't move
     My occupants always complain,
     But if I move and don't stand still
     Then I can usually make them be silent.

230. In daytime I have nothing to do
And am left quietly in a corner.
But at night I'm brought out
And swallow fire and flame.

231. Scarcely was his father in this world
When the son could be found sitting on the roof.

232. There are four brothers in this world
That were all born together:
The first he runs and never wearies,
The second eats and is never full.
The third he drinks and is ever thirsty
And the fourth sings a song that is never good.

233. A red maiden is sitting in a green summerhouse,
If you squeeze her she will cry
And her tears they are as red as blood,
But yet her heart is made of stone.

234. There is a thing that hangs on the wall without nail or string. What
is it?

235. I'm out and about all day and yet I always stay at home.

236. Patch upon patch and never a stitch. What am I?

237. He who lacks it seeks it
He who has it mistreats it.

238. Unseasoned, uncooked and served up at no table,
Yet emperors, kings and princesses all partake of this fare.

239. Something hangs on the wall that was made by no hand.
Untouched it was made without hands, without tools. He who can
solve my riddle may sleep with me this night.

240. I sat and I ate and from me one ate,
And below me one ate and above me one ate.
Tell me good sir what is that?

241. I died without being born
And married my father when I was only a day old,
Yet I never had a mother. Who am I?

242. A cloud was my mother,
The wind is my father,
My son is the cool stream
And my daughter is the fruit of the land.
A rainbow is my bed,
The earth my final resting place
And I'm the torment of man.

243. In a corner on the wall
     I lie in wait for my prey
     Without fists or firearms.
     I stretch my nets around me
     And my table is seldom bare.

244. My fatherland is Arabia,
     Though in England they roast me brown.
     I'm ground up inside a mill
     And tortured with scalding water
     And then they pour milk over me
     And drink me at their leisure.

245. First I was a plant, then I was dust,
     Then I was locked up in gold, silver or tin –
     Each according to his whim.
     To some I am a nuisance,
     To others indispensable.

246. First I was burnt, then I was beaten,
     Then I was drowned and pierced with nails.
     What am I?

247. Poke your fingers in my eyes,
     And I will open wide my jaws.
     Linen cloth, quills or paper
     My greedy lust devours it all.

248. There is a white egg in a green house,
     And if you break open the house you can take the egg out.
     But I tell you to a man, no bird ever laid it.

249. The sun cooked it, the hand broke it off,
     The foot trod on it and the mouth enjoyed it.

250. There is a man lies buried deep,
     His grave spread all around him,
     He was not in heaven, he was not on earth,
     Where can that man be found?

251. It has four legs but cannot run.
     It has many feathers but cannot fly
     And always stands as quiet as a mouse.

252. Why is a good meerschaum like a water-colour artist?

253. Lives without a body, hears without ears, speaks without mouth,
     to which the air alone gives birth.

254. Why is O the noisiest of the vowels?

255. Without as smooth as glass,
     Within a woolly mass.
     But hid amid the wool
     There lurks a nice mouthful.

256. A pitcher with a thousand chinks,
     Yet ne'er lets out the water it drinks.

257. My back as frying-pan does appear;
         Beneath a snowy breast;
     A pair of scissors jut in the rear;
         What am I? Have you guessed?

258. I keep a tiny something in a tiny box,
     Secured under many keys and many locks:
     If the tiny something breaketh loose,
     Of the tiny box what is the use?

259. He feeds on beef the livelong day,
     At night he scans the Milky Way.

260. Though it is not an ox, it has horns; though it is not an ass, it has a
     pack-saddle; and wherever it goes it leaves silver behind. What is
     it?

261. I bind it, and it walks; I loose it, and it stops.

262. A messenger that could not speak, bearing a letter that was not
     written, came to a city that had no foundations.

263. There was a man o' Adam's race,
     He had a certain dwalling-place;
     It was neither in heeven, earth, nor hell –
     Tell me where this man did dwell!

264. Hair without, and hair within,
     A' hair, and nae skin.

265. A beautiful lady in a garden was laid,
         Her beauty was fair as the sun,
     In one hour of her life she became a man's wife,
         And she died before she was born.

266. The first letter of our fore-fadyr,
     A worker of wax,
     An I and an N;
     The colour of an ass:
     And what have you then?

267. In the middle of the garden was a river,
     In the middle of the river was a boat,
     In the middle of the boat was a lady,

Who wore a red petticoat.
Eve ye dinna ken her name
It's yer ain self to blame,
'Cause I telt ye in the middle of the riddle.

268. There is a word in the English language the first two letters of
which signify a male, the first three a female, the first four a great
man, the whole a great woman.

269. I am become of flesh and blood,
    As other creatures be;
Yet there's neither flesh nor blood
    Doth remain in me.
I make kings that they fall out,
    I make them agree;
And yet there's neither flesh nor blood
    Doth remain in me.

ANTIPHANES (4th century BC)

Ancient Greek dramatist. Riddle cited in Athenaeus's *Deipnosophistae*.

270. There is a feminine being which keeps its babes safe beneath its
bosom; they, though voiceless, raise a cry sonorous over the waves
of the sea and across all the dry land, reaching what mortals they
desire, and they may hear even when they are not there; but their
sense of hearing is dull.

APOLLONIUS OF TYRE, The History of (9th century)

Popular medieval romance; versions in *Gesta Romanorum* and Gower's
Confessio Amantis (1390). Riddles taken from Spanish edition, *El Libro di
Apolonio* (13th century).

271. . . . Tell me now this thing.
What house is always murmuring,
Though the indwellers all are dumb?
Now please me with the answer. Come!

272. The river's kin and friend am I.
My lovely hair I raise on high.
My trade is to make black of white.
That one is hard to solve aright.

273. I am the forest's child most swift.
Furrows I cut and leave no rift.
I fight the winds. I'm dangerous.

274. I have no limbs, no parts inside,
But two teeth like an elephant goad.
The one who bears me I hold still.

275. I'm soft as wool, soft as a bog.
     When I swell up, I'm like a frog.
     I grow in water, where I plunge.

276. I am not black, nor white nor red;
     No tongue by which wise saws are said
     Have I. I win when I am opposite.
     I can be bought for a small bit.

ARISTOPHANES (c. 450–c. 385 BC)
Ancient Greek comic dramatist. Riddle found in *Wasps*.

277. What is that brute which throws away its shield
     Alike in air, in ocean, in the field?

AUSTEN, Jane (1775–1817)
English novelist. Riddles appear in *Emma*.

278. My first displays the wealth and pomp of kings,
         Lords of the earth! their luxury and ease.
     Another view of man, my second brings,
         Behold him there, the monarch of the seas!

     But ah! united what reverse we have!
         Man's boasted power and freedom, all are flown:
     Lord of the earth and sea, he bends a slave,
         And woman, lovely woman, reigns alone.

     Thy ready wit the word will soon supply,
         May its approval beam in that soft eye!

BEDE, The Venerable (AD 673–735)
English historian and scholar. Riddles attributed to him occur in
Excerptiones patrum, collectanea, flores ex diversis, quaestiones et parabolae
('Flores') and *Jocoseria*.

279. Tell me, I beg you, who is the woman who offers her breasts to
     countless sons, and who, however much she is sucked, pours out
     as much?

280. Tell me, what is it that fills the sky and the whole earth and tears up
     new shoots, and shakes all foundations, but cannot be seen by eyes
     or touched by hands?

281. What is it that bore me as a mother and soon will be born from me?

282. I am sitting above a horse which was not born, whose mother I
     hold in my hand.

BERNE RIDDLES, The (7th century)

Collection of sixty-two riddles from Bobbio, Italy, believed to have been written by Tullius, an Irish monk.

283. *Mortem ego pater libens adsumo pro natis*
  Et tormenta simul, cara ne pignora tristem.
  Mortuum me cuncti gaudent habere parentes
  Et sepultum nullus paruo uel funere plangit.

(I, as father, freely take up sad death for my son's sake, and torments too, lest my children suffer. All parents rejoice to have me dead and none laments at my burial with its tiny funeral.)

284. *Mortua maiorem quam uiuens porto laborem.*
  Dum iaceo, multos seruo; si stetero, paucos.
  Viscera si mihi foris detracta patescant,
  Vitam fero cunctis uictumque confero multis.
  Bestia defuncta quae nulla . . . memordit,
  Et onusta currens uiam nec planta depingo.

(I carry a greater load dead than alive. While I lie, I serve many men: if I were to stand, I should serve few. If my entrails are torn out to lie open out of doors, I bring life to all, and I give sustenance to many. A lifeless creature which . . . bites nothing, when loaded down I run on my way yet never show my feet.)

285. *Nullam ante tempus lustri genero prolem*
  Annisque peractis superbos genero natos,
  Quos domare quisquis ualet industria paruus,
  Cum eos marinus iunctus percusserit imber,
  Asperi nam lenes sic creant filii nepotes,
  Tenebris ut lucem reddant, dolori salutem.

(I shall bear no offspring before the lustral period of five years, and when the time has passed I shall bear superb sons; anyone who can make some small exertion will be strong enough to tame them, as soon as some sea storm has come and shaken them thoroughly. And thus rough sons will bring forth gentle grandsons, to give light for those in darkness and health for the afflicted.)

286. *Dissimilem sibi me mater concipit infra,*
  Et nullo uirili creata de semine fundor.
  Dum nascor sponte, gladio diuellor a uentre.
  Caesa uiuit mater: ego nam flammis aduror.
  Nullum clara manens possum concedere quaestum
  Plurimum fero lucrum, nigro si corpore mutor.

(My mother conceived me below, a different thing from herself, and I poured forth created by no male seed. While I was born spontaneously, I was torn from her belly by a sword. But my mother lives on, though cleft open, for I cauterize all wounds. I bring most profit if I am changed to having a black body.)

BIBLE, The
Judaeo-Christian religious text. Riddles occur in Proverbs, Judges, *et passim*. Those cited are from Proverbs 30.

287. Three things there are which will never be satisfied,
    four which never say, 'Enough!':
    The grave and a barren womb,
    a land thirsty for water
    and fire that never says, 'Enough!'

Three things there are which are too wonderful for me,
    four which I do not understand:
    the way of a vulture in the sky,
    the way of a serpent on the rock,
    the way of a ship out at sea,
    and the way of a man with a girl.

At three things the earth shakes,
    four things it cannot bear:
    a slave turned king,
    a churl gorging himself,
    a woman unloved when she is married,
    and a slave-girl displacing her mistress.

Four things there are which are smallest on earth
    yet wise beyond the wisest:
    ants, a people with no strength
    yet they prepare their store of food in the summer;
    rock-badgers, a feeble folk,
    yet they make their home among the rocks;
    locusts, which have no king,
    yet they sally forth in detachments;
    the lizard, which can be grasped in the hand,
    yet is found in the palaces of kings.

Three things there are which are stately in their stride,
    four which are stately as they move:
    the lion, a hero among beasts,
    which will not turn tail for anyone;
    the strutting cock and the he-goat;
    and a king going forth to lead his army.

BOILEAU (DESPRÉAUX), Nicolas (1636–1711)

French literary critic and poet. Riddle contained in a letter to Brossette (1703) but composed in 1652.

288. *Du repos des Humains implacable Ennemie,*
J'ay rendu mille Amans envieux de mon sort;
Je me repais de sang, et je trouve ma vie
Dans les bras de celui qui recherche ma mort.

(Implacable enemy of human rest, I have made a thousand lovers jealous of my lot; I feast on blood, and find my life in the arms of those who seek my death.)

BOOK OF MEERY RIDDLES, The (1629)

Anonymous riddle collection printed in London.

289. He went to the wood and caught it;
He sate him downe and sought it;
Because he could not finde it,
Home with him he brought it.

290. What work is that: the faster ye worke, [the] longer it is ere ye have done; and the slower ye worke, the sooner ye make an end?

291. What is that that is rough within, and red without,
and bristled like a bares snowt:
there is never a Lady in this Land
but will be content to take it in her hand.

292. What Kings, Queenes, and their servants be they that be burnt once a yeere, and be cut and torne as small as flesh to pot?

293. Three prisoners, such as it was,
were shut up in a prison of a glasse.
The prison doore was made of bread,
and yet they were for hunger dead.

294. Who bare the best burthen that ever was borne at any time since, or at any time before?

295. What is the most profitable beast, and that men eat least on?

296. What is that one seeketh for, and would not finde?

297. What is that:
as high as a hall,
as bitter as gall,
as soft as silke,
as white as milke?

298. What is he that getteth his living backward?

299. What is it that goeth to the water, and leaveth his guts at home?

300. Ten men's strength, and ten men's length, and ten men cannot set
it on end; yet one man may beare it.

301. Thorow a rocke, thorow a reele,
thorow an old spinning wheele,
thorow a hard shining bone:
such a riddle you have none.

302. Downe in a meddow I have 2 swine; the more meat I give them the
lowder they cry, the lesse meat I give them the stiller they lye.

303. Beyond the sea there is an oake,
and in that oake there is a nest,
and in the nest there is an egge,
and in that egge there is a yolke,
which cals together Christian folke.

304. I consume my mother that bare me,
I eat my nurse that fed me,
then I dye leaving all blinde that saw me.

BOOKE OF MERRIE RIDDLES, A (1631)

Anonymous riddle collection printed in London for Robert Bird. Also
known as *Prettie Riddles*.

305. A maid there was that married a man, by whom was many
children gotten; yet all they died, and went away, before the
mother was begotten.

306. In what place crew the cock so lowd,
that all men heard it out of doubt?

307. When I am old, I cast my skinne,
whereby I doe come young againe.

308. White I am, and blacke withall,
I have eyes, and yet am blind.
Gaine and losse not without braule
I doe procure, as you shall find.

309. I am within as white as snow,
without as greene as hearbs that grow;
I am higher then a house,
and yet am lesser then a mouse.

310. There dwels foure sisters near this town,
in favour like, and like in gowne.
When they run for a prise to win,
all at once they doe begin.
One runnes as fast as doth the other,
yet cannot overtake each other.

311. Sixe haires did come within a plain,
     whom hounds had started out the nest.
     Hill up, hill downe they runne amaine,
     till they were weary and then did rest.
     They caught him once, and scapt again,
     more eager went they then before,
     and tooke more paine then (as I win)
     to beare away the game and more.
     The hounds and hunters all were one,
     each liked his game and took his prey.
     But when their sport was past and done,
     they left their haires and came away.

312. In open field I cannot lye,
     and yet may rest quietly
     within a boxe of ivory.

313. A ship there drives upon the tide,
     that sailes doth beare, she hath no mast.
     But one oare she hath on each side;
     her sailes the snow in whitenesse passe.
     In her front weares two lanthorns bright;
     but when she is upon point to fall,
     then lend an eare, for great delight
     of musicke she affords to all.

314. What man is he of wit so base,
     that wears both his eyes in a case;
     for feare of hurting them it is,
     and I doe find it not amisse.

315. My prey I seek the fields and weeds about,
     and have more teeth then beasts within the land,
     and whensoever my game I have found out,
     then safe I bring it to my master's hand.
     Upon my back the deere he layes
     and there doth kill one, sometimes more:
     he shuts me up and goes his wayes,
     better contented then before.

316. A tree there is that boughes doth beare
     in number five, as I doe know:
     no equall length they never were,
     and on their tops doe hornes grow.
     Yet they are tied about with gold,
     except the longest, without doubt,
     which for use sake might be controld,
     if it with gold were hoopt about.

317. In what place of the earth doth the skie seeme
    to be no larger then a yard, or twaine?
    Which? I pray thee,
    tell mee.

318. What doth with his roote upwards grow,
    and downward with his head doth show?

319. What is lesser then a mouse,
    and hath more windows then a house?

320. When we by the way do goe,
    upon our shoulders we beare our way;
    if we were not, then many should be
    wet to the skin in a rayny day.

321. In the last minute of my age
    I doe waxe young againe.
    And have so still continued,
    since world did first begin.

322. Trip trap in a gap,
    as many feete as a hundred sheepe.

323. I know a child borne by my mother,
    naturall borne as other children be,
    that is neither my sister nor my brother.
    Answer me shortly: what is he?

324. I have a smith without a hand,
    he workes the worke that no man can.
    He serves our God, and doth man ease
    without any fire in his furnace.

325. As round as a hoope I am,
    most part when it is day;
    but being night, then am I long
    as any snake, I say.

326. What is it [that] more eyes doth weare
    then forty men within the land,
    which glister as the christall cleare
    against the sunne, when they doe stand?

327. My coate is greene, and I can prate
    of divers things about my grate.
    In such a prison I am set
    that hath more loope holes then a net.

BOTTINI, Giovanna Statira (d. 1727)

Pseudonym (anagram) of Giovanni Battista Taroni. Riddles published in *Cento nodi* (1718).

328. *Quel, che m'ha in odio, ognor mi va cercando,*
   E da quel, che mi cerca io sempre fuggo,
   Senza timor di qua, di là volando
   E gigli e rose ogn'or lambisco e suggo:
   Per le vie più segrete io vado errando,
   E chi mi nutre ingratamente io struggo,
   Ma a forza di rotture al fine esangue
   In man di chi mel diede io rendo il sangue.

(He who hates me is always searching for me, and from he who searches for me, I am always fleeing, without fear, flying here and there. Lilies and roses I always glide over and suck: I wander through the most secret ways, and, ungratefully, I destroy that which nourishes me. But finally bloodless because of being broken I render the blood into the hand of he who gave it me.)

329. *Ardito, senza brando, e quasi ignudo*
   Quante volte fugai le armate schiere;
   Fui del Duce primier sostegno, e scudo,
   Portai spoglie nemiche, armi, e bandiere;
   Pugnai ne' boschi ancor contro il più crudo
   Furor de' mostri, e di voraci fiere,
   E per unico vanto il Ciel mi diede
   Tutte le glorie, e le fortune al piede.

(Bold, without a sword, and almost naked, how many times have I escaped from armed bands. I was the prime support and shield of the chief, I carried enemy spoils, arms and flags. I still fought in the woods against the most vicious fury of monsters, and of voracious wild beasts, and, as a unique honour, Heaven gave me all glory and fortune at my feet.)

CARROLL, Lewis (1832–1898)

Pseudonym of Charles Lutwidge Dodgson, English writer and mathematician. Riddles contained in *Through the Looking Glass* (1872) and miscellaneous journals, etc.

330.   'First the fish must be caught.'
   That is easy: a baby, I think, could have caught it.
      'Next, the fish must be bought.'
   That is easy: a penny, I think, would have bought it.

'Now cook me the fish!'
That is easy, and will not take more than a minute.
   'Let it lie in a dish!'
That is easy, because it is already in it.

   'Bring it here! Let me sup!'
It is easy to set such a dish on the table.
   'Take the dish-cover up!'
Ah, *that* is so hard that I fear I'm unable!

   For it holds it like glue –
Holds the lid to the dish, while it lies in the middle:
   Which is easiest to do,
Un-dish-cover the fish, or dishcover the riddle?

331.
I. My First

The air is bright with hues of light,
   And rich with laughter and with singing:
Young hearts beat high in ecstasy,
   And banners wave, and bells are ringing:
But silence falls with falling day,
And there's an end to mirth and play.
     Ah, well-a-day!

II. My Second

Rest your old bones, ye ancient crones!
   The kettle sings, the firelight dances:
Deep be it quaffed, the magic draught
   That fills the soul with golden fancies:
For youth and pleasance will not stay,
And ye are withered, worn, and gray.
     Ah, well-a-day!

III. My Whole

O fair cold face! O form of grace,
   For human passion madly yearning!
O weary air of dumb despair,
   From marble won, to marble turning!
'Leave us not thus!' we fondly pray.
'We cannot let thee pass away!'
     Ah, well-a-day!

332. They both make a roaring, a roaring all night:
They both are a fisherman-father's delight:
They are both, when in fury, a terrible sight!

The first nurses tenderly three little hulls,
To the lullaby-music of shrill-screaming gulls,
And laughs when they dimple his face with their skulls.

The second's a tidyish sort of a lad,
Who behaves pretty well to a man he calls 'Dad',
And earns the remark, 'Well, he isn't so bad!'

Of the two put together, oh, what shall I say?
Tis a time when 'to live' means the same as 'to play':
When the busiest person does nothing all day.

When the grave College Don, full of love inexpressi-
Ble, puts it all by, and is forced to confess he
Can think but of Agnes and Evie and Jessie.

333. A monument – men all agree –
Am I in all sincerity,
    Half cat, half hindrance made.
If head and tail removed should be,
Then most of all you strengthen me;
Replace my head, the stand you see
    On which my tail is laid.

CERVANTES SAAVEDRA, Miguel de (1547–1616)

Spanish novelist and dramatist. Riddles contained in *La Galatea* (1585).

334. What is that powerful thing
Which, from the orient to the drooping west
Is known and is renowned?
Now strong and valiant,
Now timorous and weak,
Taking and giving health,
Virtue both shows and conceals
In more than a single time.
Stronger is in age,
And in the cheerful growth,
Changeth it doth in that which changeth not.
By some unusual pre-eminence
It makes him tremble who perspires,
And for the rarest eloquence
Can it to baseness and to silence turn.
With divers means,
It measures its being and its appellation,
Is wont to seize renown,
Such as is known in lands innumerable.
Armless itself, it yet subdues the armed,
And to be victorious is compelled,
Seeming directly vengeance to pursue
The most disgraced is,
A thing of wonder is it,

Which in field and city,
At the head of proof,
That any man may boldness feel,
Yet doth in the scuffle lose.

335. Who is that which all eyes is,
From the crown to the feet.
Occasionally his own interest without,
Is cause of amorous annoyances?
Accustomed is he quarrels to appease,
Yet neither goes nor comes,
And though possessing eyes so many,
Few children doth discover,
Of grief bearing the name,
Which is accounted mortal,
Both good and harm he doth,
Love moderates and inflames.

336. Dark 'tis, yet very clear,
Containing infinite variety,
Encumbering us with truths,
Which are at length declared.
'Tis sometimes of a jest produced,
At others of high fancy,
And it is wont defiance to create,
Of airy matters treating.

Any man its name may know,
Even to little children,
Many there are, and masters have
In different ways.
There is no old woman it embraces not,
With of these ladies, one
At times in good odour,
This tires, that satisfies.

Wise ones there be who overwatch
Sensations to extract.
Some run wild
The more they watch o'er it.
Such is foolish, and such curious,
Such easy, such complex,
Yet, be it something, be it nought,
Reveal to me what the said thing may be?

337. What is that which to its displeasure
     Measures its feet by its eyes,
     Without discomfort causing,
     Making them quickly sing?
     It is pleasant to extract them,
     Though ofttimes he who them fairly extracts,
     Not only does not his sure ill assuage,
     But more disgust conceals.

338. Fire bites, and the mouthful
     Is the damage, and the profit of the masticator,
     The wounded wight loses no blood,
     Though he should be well slashed.
     But if the wound is deep,
     Its point the hand not hitting,
     Death to the stricken party doth ensue,
     And in that death stands life.

CHOICE COLLECTION OF RIDDLES, CHARADES, REBUSSES, A (1792)

339. In a garden was laid
        A most beautiful maid
     As ever was seen in the morn;
        She was made a wife
        The first day of her life,
     And died before she was born.

CHRISTOPHORUS of Mytilene (*fl.* 1050)
Byzantine poet and enigmatographer.

340. You seized me and yet I fled; you see me flee and cannot hold me
     tight; you press me in your hand but I escape and your fist is left
     empty.

CLARETUS, Dr (14th century)
Bohemian monk. Riddles appear in untitled MS.

341. Like grass it is green, but it is not grass
     Like blood it is red, but it is not blood.
     It is round and smooth like an egg.

342. It's small and sweet and comes in a bony pot.

343. What flies without flesh?

344. The ox is entering the stable, and has left his horns outside.

345. What dies and always gives birth?

346. A vessel have I,
   That is round as a pear,
   Moist in the middle,
   Surrounded with hair;
   And often it happens
   That water flows there.

347. Who gives what he does not have?

348. Three hundred and sixty-five birds, twelve griffins, and three nests, together produce but a single egg.

349. What did the whole world hear?

350. What enters a room without any noise, without using the door?

351. What grows in the field without roots?

352. Inside the wall, when it is cooked, you will find two kinds of nut.

353. The thing I have is male and wrinkled, and the ladies love it.

354. If I drive out all the sheep, I can milk the fold.

355. It is hairy round about, it is pretty in the middle, but at the bottom it wears a little thorn.

356. In cavern moist my flesh doth lie,
   And with this wriggling piece pray I.

357. A layman comes with an iron spoon, shoves it in and opens up his mother; he salts her, and sews up her skin; then he takes his mother's children, grinds all their bones, and feeds his own children.

358. Here hangs a shaven one; if you were to put a hairy one beneath, the hairy one would want the shaven one.

CLEOBULUS (*fl. c.* 600 BC)
Ancient Greek poet. Riddle cited in *Greek Anthology* and Diogenes Laertius's *Lives of Eminent Philosophers*.

359. There is one father and twelve children. Each of these has twice thirty children of different aspect; some of them we see to be white and the others black, and though immortal, they all perish.

COWPER, William (1731–1800)
English poet. This riddle, written in July 1780, appeared in *The Gentleman's Magazine* for December 1806.

360. I am just two and two, I am warm, I am cold,
   And the parent of numbers that cannot be told.
   I am lawful, unlawful – a duty, a fault,

I am often sold dear, good for nothing when bought;
     An extraordinary boon, and a matter of course,
     And yielded with pleasure when taken by force.

CROCE, Giulio Cesare (1550–1609)

Italian blacksmith-poet. Riddles published in *Notte sollazzevole di cento enigmi* (1599) and *Seconde notte sollazzevole di cento enigmi* (1601).

361. *In verde selva nacqui, e a l'aria, al vento,*
     Come volle mia sorte, un tempo stetti;
     E del mio stato mi vivea contento,
     Nè mai mi lamentai in fatti, o in detti;
     Ma poi tagliato con pena, e tormento,
     A corpo vuoto fo diversi effetti,
     Che mentre per lo naso m'è soffiato
     Grido, e per gl'occhi fuor rimando il fiato.

(I was born in a green wood, and in the open air and in the wind, it was my fate for me to stay for a time; and I was happy to live in my state. Nor did I ever complain in word or in deed; but then cut down with hurt and torment, with an empty body I produce various effects, such that when my nose is blown into I shout, and I send out my breath through my eyes.)

362. *Io sono al mondo tanto sventurato,*
     che quasi non vorrei esser nasciuto;
     poi che, misero me, son bastonato
     in vita, e in morte ogn'hor pesto e battuto;
     pur tanta contentezza hò in simil stato,
     ch'io fo tacer la cetra, & il liuto:
     e mentre ch'un mi batte, e mi martella,
     col ferro altri si foran le budella.

(I am so unfortunate in the world that I almost wish that I had never been born; since, unhappy me, I am beaten in my life, and in death kicked and hit every hour. Yet I am so content in such a state, that I silence the zither and the lute. And whilst one is hitting and hammering me, others have their entrails punched with iron.)

363. *Sospesa in aria stò, nè tocco nulla,*
     E circondata son di lumi intorno,
     Hor di novo mi vesto, hora son brulla,
     E al caldo, al freddo stò la notte, e'l giorno,
     Ogn'un di calpestarmi si trastulla,
     Fino alle bestie mi fan danno, e scorno,
     E tai tesori ascondo nel mio seno,
     Che chi gli trova fò felice a pieno.

(I am suspended in the air, I touch nothing, and I am surrounded by lights. Now I dress myself afresh, and now I am naked, and I am in the heat and the cold, by night and by day. Everyone amuses himself by trampling upon me, even the animals abuse and scorn me, and yet I have such treasures hidden in my bosom that he who finds them I can make full of happiness.)

DAVIES, Sir John (1569–1626)
Solicitor-General for Ireland, poet and author of a number of acrostics. Also wrote riddles.

364. There was a man bespake a thing,
Which when the owner home did bring,
He that made it did refuse it:
And he that brought it would not use it,
And he that hath it doth not know
Whether he hath it yea or no.

DEMAUNDES JOYOUS, The (1511)
Anonymous translation and selection from the French *Demandes joyeuses en manière de quodlibets* (c. 1500). Printed by Wynkyn de Worde.

365. Which is the broadest water and least jeopardy to pass over?

366. Why come dogs so often to the church?

367. Why doth a dog turn him thrice about ere he lieth him down?

368. What thing is it that hath horns at the arse?

369. What is it that freezeth never?

370. What thing is it, the less it is the more it is dread?

371. Wherefore is it that young children weep as soon as ever they be born?

372. What time in the year beareth the goose most feathers?

373. What was he that slew the fourth part of the world?

374. What thing is that which hath no end?

DES ACCORDS, Éstienne Tabourot (1549–90)
French lawyer and poet. A number of *rébus de Picardie* and literary rebuses appear in *Les Bigarrures du Seigneur des Accords* (1582).

375. *G a c o b i a l*

376. *ooooo eeee sont aaaaa pons*

377. *trop   vent   bien*
tils   sont   pris

378. *hait   en   tient*
    le   pens   le coeur

379. *G a p pour mes aa*
    d tenter

380. *comme* 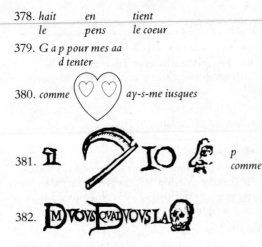 *ay-s-me iusques*

381. *p*
    comme

382.

383. *Pri-bonne-se pren-fait bon-dre*

DIALOGUE OF SALOMON AND SATURNUS, The (14th century)

384. Tell me, who was he that was never born, was then buried in his mother's womb, and after death was baptized?

385. Tell me, what is the heaviest thing on earth to bear?

386. Tell me, what is that which pleaseth one man and displeaseth another?

387. Tell me, what are the four things that never were and never will be full?

EUBULUS (*fl.* 4th century BC)

Ancient Greek poet and dramatist. Riddle cited in Athenaeus's *Deipnosophistae*.

388. It has no tongue, yet it talks, its name is the same for male or female, steward of its own winds, hairy, or sometimes hairless; saying things unintelligible to them that understand, drawing out one melody after another; one thing it is, yet many, and if one wound it, it is unwounded. Tell me, what is it? Why are you puzzled?

389. I know one that is heavy when he is young, and when he becomes old, though wingless, he lightly flies and leaves the land invisible.

125

EUSEBIUS (d. 747)

Abbot of Wearmouth. Riddles published with those of Tatwine (q.v.).

390. By nature I am simple and have no wisdom in any way, but now
every wise man will follow my tracks; now I dwell on earth,
erewhile I roamed on high through the heavens; I am white in
appearance, though I leave black traces.

391. *Per me mors adquiritur et bona vita tenetur.*
Me multi fugiunt, multique frequenter adorant;
Sumque timenda malis, non sum tamen horrida justis.
Damnavi virum, sic multos carcere solvi.

(Through me death is acquired and good life is maintained. Many
flee me, and many frequently worship me; I am to be feared by bad
men, but I am not terrifying to the just. I have condemned a man
and thus released many from prison.)

EXETER BOOK, The (10th century)

Anglo-Saxon miscellany presented to Exeter Cathedral in 1072. Riddles
once believed to have been the work of the Anglo-Saxon poet
Cynewulf.

392. In former days my father and mother
Abandoned me a dead thing lacking breath,
Or life or being. Then one began,
A kinswoman kind, to care for, and love me;
Covered me with her clothing, wrapped me in her raiment,
With the same affection she felt for her own;
Until, by the law of my life's shaping,
Under an alien bosom I quickened with breath.
My foster mother fed me thereafter
Until I grew sturdy and strengthened for flight.
Then of her dear ones, of daughters and sons,
She had the fewer for what she did.

393. By foot I travel, and I tear the earth,
The grassy fields, as long as I have life.
But when my spirit leaves me I bind fast
The dark Welsh slaves or sometimes better men.
Sometimes I give a noble warrior
Drink from my breast; sometimes the haughty bride
Treads on me. Sometimes the dark-haired Welsh maid
Brought from afar carries and presses me,
A foolish drunken girl at dark of night
Wets me with water, sometimes pleasantly
Warms me beside the fire, sticks in my bosom
Her wanton hand, constantly turns me round,

Strokes me all night. Tell me what I am called,
That while I live may plunder all the land,
And after death give service to mankind.

394. My beak is below, I burrow and nose
Under the ground. I go as I'm guided
By my master the farmer, old foe of the forest;
Bent and bowed, at my back he walks,
Forward pushing me over the field;
Sows on my path where I've passed along.
I came from the wood, a wagon carried me;
I was fitted with skill, I am full of wonders.
As grubbing I go, there's green on one side,
But black on the other my path is seen.
A curious prong pierces my back;
Beneath me in front, another grows down
And forward pointing is fixed to my head.
I tear and gash the ground with my teeth,
If my master steer me with skill from behind.

395. I'm a strange creature, for I satisfy women,
a service to the neighbours! No one suffers
at my hands except for my slayer.
I grow very tall, erect in a bed,
I'm hairy underneath. From time to time
a beautiful girl, the brave daughter
of some churl dares to hold me,
grips my russet skin, robs me of my head
and puts me in the pantry. At once that girl
with plaited hair who has confined me
remembers our meeting. Her eye moistens.

396. I'm prized by men, in the meadows I'm found,
Gathered on hill-sides, and hunted in groves;
From dale and from down, by day I am brought.
Airy wings carry me, cunningly store me,
Hoarding me safe. Yet soon men take me;
Drained into vats, I'm dangerous grown.
I tie up my victim, and trip him, and throw him;
Often I floor a foolish old churl.
Who wrestles with me, and rashly would measure
His strength against mine, will straightway find himself
Flung to the ground, flat on his back,
Unless he leave his folly in time,
Put from his senses and power of speech,
Robbed of his might, bereft of his mind,

Of his hands and feet. Now find me my name,
Who can bind and enslave men so upon earth,
And bring fools low in broad daylight.

397. There's a troop of tiny folk travelling swift,
Brought by the breeze o'er the brink of the hill,
Buzzing black-coated bold little people –
Noisy musicians; well-known is their song.
They scour the thickets, but sometimes invade
The rooms of the town. Now tell me their names.

398. Wounded I am, and weary with fighting;
Gashed by the iron, gored by the point of it,
Sick of battle-work, battered and scarred.
Many a fearful fight have I seen, when
Hope there was none, or help in the thick of it,
Ere I was down and fordone in the fray.
Offspring of hammers, hardest of battle-blades,
Smithied in forges, fell on me savagely,
Doomed to bear the brunt and the shock of it,
Fierce encounter of clashing foes.
Leech cannot heal my hurts with his simples,
Salves for my sores have I sought in vain.
Blade-cuts dolorous, deep in the side of me,
Daily and nightly redouble my wounds.

399. A strange thing hangs by man's hip,
hidden by a garment. It has a hole
in its head. It is stiff and strong
and its firm bearing reaps a reward.
When the retainer hitches his clothing
high above his knee, he wants the head
of that hanging thing to find the old hole
that it, outstretched, has often filled before.

400. I'm told a certain object grows
in the corner, rises and expands, throws up
a crust. A proud wife carried off
that boneless wonder, the daughter of a king
covered that swollen thing with a cloth.

401. A moth ate a word! To me that seemed
A strange thing to happen, when I heard that wonder –
A worm that would swallow the speech of a man,
Sayings of strength steal in the dark,
Thoughts of the mighty; yet the thieving sprite
Was none the wiser for the words he had eaten!

402. I war with the wind, with the waves I wrestle;
    I must battle with both when the bottom I seek,
    My strange habitation by surges o'er-roofed.
    I am strong in the strife, while still I remain;
    As soon as I stir, they are stronger than I.
    They wrench and they wrest, till I run from my foes;
    What was put in my keeping they carry away.
    If my back be not broken, I baffle them still;
    The rocks are my helpers, when hard I am pressed;
    Grimly I grip them. Guess what I'm called.

403. My robe is silent, when I rest on earth,
    Or run by the shore, or ruffle the pools;
    But oft on my pinions upward I mount,
    Borne to the skies on the buoyant air,
    High o'er the haunts and houses of men,
    Faring afar with the fleeting clouds.
    Then sudden my feathers are filled with music.
    They sing in the wind, as I sail aloft
    O'er wave and wood, a wandering sprite.

404. I was an armèd warrior, but now
    The youthful courtier covers my proud neck
    With twisted filigree of gold and silver.
    Sometimes I'm kissed by heroes, and again
    I woo to battle with my melody
    Comrades in full accord. At times the courser
    Bears me across the border, and again
    Over the floods the stallion of the sea
    Conveys me radiant with ornaments.
    Sometimes a maiden, garlanded with jewels,
    Brims full my winding bosom, and again
    Perforce I lie – hard, headless, solitary
    Upon the board. Sometimes, set off with trappings,
    In comely guise upon the wall I hang
    Where heroes drink. Again, horsed warriors
    On forays wear me, glorious apparel;
    Then, dappled with gold, I must inspire the wind
    From some one's bosom. Whilom stately men
    I summon to banquetings and wine; sometimes
    My voice resounds with freedom to the captive,
    Flight to the foe. Now find out what I'm called.

405. I saw a creature in the homes of men
    Which feeds the cattle. It has many teeth.
    Its beak is useful to it. It points downwards.

It plunders gently and goes home again,
Wanders among the mounds and seeks out herbs.
It always finds out those that are not firm.
It lets the fair ones stand upon their roots,
Firm, undisturbed in their established place,
And brightly shine and blossom and grow tall.

EZRA, Abraham ibn (1089–1164)
Spanish Hebrew poet and grammarian from Cordova.

406. There was a she-mule in my house: I opened the door, and she became a heifer.

407. Take thirty from thirty and the remainder is sixty.

EZRA, Moses ibn (c. 1070–c. 1138)
Spanish Hebrew philosopher, linguist and poet. Wrote occasional riddles.

408. What is the sister of the sun, though made for the night? The fire causes her tears to fall, and when she is near dying they cut off her head.

FANSHAWE, Catherine Maria (1765–1834)
English poet. Best remembered for the following riddle, once mistakenly ascribed to Lord Byron.

409. 'Twas whispered in heaven, 'twas muttered in hell,
And echo caught faintly the sound as it fell;
On the confines of earth 'twas permitted to rest,
And the depth of the ocean its presence confessed . . .
Yet in shade let it rest, like a delicate flower,
Ah, breathe on it softly, – it dies in an hour.

FIRDUSI or FIRDAUSI (c. 950–1020)
Pseudonym of Abul Qasim Mansur, Persian poet. Riddles occur in the epic *Shanamah*.

410. Twelve cypresses stand in a circle and shine in resplendent green; each has thirty branches, and neither their esteem nor their number becomes less in the land of the Parsees.

411. There are two splendid horses, one black as pitch, the other of shining crystal; each runs ahead of the other but never catches it.

412. There is a green garden full of birds; a man with a large scythe goes about it, busily mowing green and dry plants; neither complaints nor submission to his will divert him from his purpose. There two cypresses rise from the waves of the sea like reeds; a bird has its

nest in them. When it is sitting in them, there is a fragrance like musk. One of the trees is always green and bears fruit, the other is wilting.

FOX, Charles James (1749–1806)
English Whig statesman. Credited with occasional enigmas.

413. I went to the Crimea; I stopped there, and I never went there, and I came back again.

414. My *first* is expressive of no disrespect,
But I never call you by it when you are by;
If my *second* you still are resolved to reject,
As dead as my *whole*, I shall presently lie.

GALILEI, Galileo (1564–1642)
Italian scientist. Wrote occasional riddles.

415. *Mostro son io più strano, è più difforme*
    Che l'Arpia, la Sirena, o la Chimera;
    Nè in terra, in aria, in acqua è alcuna fiera,
    Ch'abbia di membra così varie forme.
Parte a parte non ho che sia conforme,
    Più che s'una sia bianca, o l'altra nera;
    Spesso di cacciator dietro ho una schiera,
    Che de' miei piè van rintracciando l'orme.
Nelle tenebre oscure è il mio soggiorno;
    Che se dall'ombre al chiaro lume passo,
    Tosto l'alma da me sen fugge, come
Sen fugge il sogno all'apparir del giorno,
    E le mie membra disunite lasso,
    E l'esser perdo con la vita, e'l nome.

(I am a monster, stranger and more alien than the Harpy, the Siren or the Chimera. Neither on land, in the air or in the sea is there a beast whose limbs can have so many shapes; no one piece of me conforms with another, anymore than if one is white, the other is black. A band of hunters often follows behind me looking for the tracks made by my feet. I inhabit the darkest places, and if I pass from the shadows into bright light my soul quickly slips away with the coming of the day and my tired limbs fall away, and I lose my being with my life and with my name.)

GIFFORD, Humphrey (fl. 1580)
Minor English poet. Riddles contained in *Posie of Gillyflowers* (1580).

416. A mightie blacke horse, with gallant white winges,
    Within his graund paunch beares many straunge things:

Hée oft doth travayle for masters avayle,
And carges his bridle tyed fast to his tayle.
In going hée flyes twixt earth and the ayre,
And oft, where they would not, his riders doth beare:
Hée hath divers eies, and yet cannot sée,
I pray you doe tell mée what may this beast bée?

417. A certaine thing liveth in place néere at hande,
Whose nature is straunge, if it bée well scand:
It sées without eyes, it flyes without winges,
It runnes without feete, it workes wondrous things.
To places far distant it often doth rome:
Yet never departeth, but taryes at home.
If thou doe it covet to féele or to sée,
Thy labour is lost, for it may not bée.

418. From south and west commeth a straunge warlike nation,
Attirde and appareld in wonderfull fashion:
In garments milke white, these people are clad,
Which strike and oppresse both good men and bad
But favour they shew in dealing their blowes,
And save him from danger, ech on his way goes.
And on his backe caryes dead bodyes great store,
Which with their thicke buffets had beate them before,
Great furies are kindled at end of the fray:
Which makes this straunge nation all vanish away.

419. A certain dead creature in mine armes I take,
With her back to my bosome, great glée doth shée make,
As thus I doe hold her, she greatly doth chéere mée,
And wel are they pleased that sée me and heare mée.
Whilst erst it remayned in forest and field,
It silent remayning, no speech forth did yéeld.
But since she of life, by death was deprived,
With language shée speaketh, mens sprites are revived.

420. Two are we in name, though in substaunce but one,
First framed by arte then finisht with mone.
Before we are ready, for those that will buy,
Through greatnesse of torment, wée howle and wée cry.
Yet féele we no griefe, for all this anoy,
Great numbers by us have comfort and ioy,
Who when for their profits we have done what wée may,
They then do reiect us, and cast us away.

132

GLAUKOS RIDDLE, The (n.d.)

Oldest recorded riddle in the Greek language, found in Apollodorus. By solving this riddle, Glaukos, son of King Minos of Crete, was restored to life by the seer Polyidos.

421. In the fields grazeth a calf whose body changeth hue thrice in the space of each day. It is first white, then red, and at the last black.

GREEK ANTHOLOGY, The

Ancient Greek miscellany. Riddles occur in Book 14.

422. I am the black child of a white father; a wingless bird, flying even to the clouds of heaven. I give birth to tears of mourning in pupils that meet me, and at once on my birth I am dissolved into air.

423. One wind, two ships, ten sailors rowing, and one steersman directs both.

424. My whole is an island; my first the lowing of a cow, and my second what a creditor says.

425. I once saw a beast running straight on its back through a wood cut by the steel, and its feet touched not the earth.

426. I alone delight in intercourse with women at their husbands' own request.

427. Slain, I slew the slayer, but even so he went not to Hades; but I died.

428. I slew my brother, my brother again slew me; our death is caused by our father, and after our death we both kill our mother.

429. There are two sisters german; one gives birth to the other, and herself having brought forth is born from the other, so that being sisters and of one blood they are actually sisters and mothers in common.

430. My name, if you add a letter to it, produces a blow of the foot, but, if not, it will never allow man's feet to stumble.

431. Only to me it is allowed to have open intercourse with women at the request of their husbands, and I alone mount young men, grown men, and old men, and virgins, while their parents grieve.

432. If you look at me I look at you too. You look with eyes, but I not with eyes, for I have no eyes. And if you like, I speak without a voice, for you have a voice, but I only have lips that open in vain.

433. Wood gave birth to me and iron reformed me, and I am the mystic receptacle of the Muses. When shut I am silent, but I speak when you unfold me. Ares alone is the confidant of my conversation.

434. I was born in the mountains and a tree was my mother; the fire was my father and I am a blackened mass. If my father melts me inside a deep vessel of clay, I protect from wounds the chariot of the sea.

435. I have nothing inside me and everything is inside me, and I grant the use of my virtue to all without charge.

436. No one sees me when he sees, but he sees me when he sees not; he who speaks not speaks, and he who runs not runs, and I am untruthful though I tell all truth.

437. If you had taken me in my youth, haply you would have drunk the blood shed from me; but now that time has finished making me old, eat me, wrinkled as I am, with no moisture in me, crushing my bones together with my flesh.

GUESS BOOK, The (c. 1820)
Chapbook printed by William Davison of Alnwick (1781–1858).

438. Made of two bodies join'd,
Without foot or hand;
And yet you will find
I can both run and stand.

439. In almost every house I'm seen,
(No wonder, then, I'm common),
I'm neither man, nor maid, nor child,
Nor yet a married woman.

440. To rich and poor we useful are;
And yet for our reward,
By both at last we're thrown away,
Without the least regard.

441. I am a busy active creature,
Fashion'd for the sport of nature,
Nimbly skip from tree to tree,
Under a well-wrought canopy;
Bid Chloe then to Mira tell
What's my name and where I dwell.

442. My sides are firmly lac'd about,
Yet nothing is within;
You'll think my head is strange indeed,
Being nothing else but skin.

HALEVI, Jehudah (c. 1086–1141)

Spanish Hebrew poet. Riddles contained in *Cuzari (Al-Khazari)*.

443. What is it that one lays naked in the grave and yet it does not suffer death, it begets children there, it cares for them attentively, until they appear fully dressed?

444. A little staff, yet of inestimable value, green in colour as if consumed by love-sorrow, a hollow body yet with a brave heart, it casts down heroes, it brings pain to many, it hastens to fill itself properly, it does not accomplish its task with empty mouth. And five servants are ready at one time, cheerfully executing its commands. Now it likes to communicate song and elegance, now it is able to soften a prince's heart, it can make peace, it can bring about war. Tell what it is, what it means.

445. What is it, then, at which our heart laughs merrily when it weeps, but makes our heart sad and mournful when it shines brightly?

446. What is it that's blind with an eye in its head,
    But the race of mankind its use cannot spare;
Spends all its life in clothing the dead,
    But always itself is naked and bare?

HERVARAR SAGA, The

Ancient Norse saga. Riddles occur in the story of Heidrek and Gestumblindi.

447. I would that I had that which I had yesterday. Guess O King, what that was: – Exhauster of men, retarder of words, yet originator of speech.

448. What was the drink that I had yesterday? It was neither wine nor water, mead nor ale, nor any kind of food; and yet I went away with my thirst quenched.

449. Who is that clanging one who traverses hard paths which he has trod before? He kisses very rapidly, has two mouths and walks on gold alone.

450. What is that huge one that passes over the earth, swallowing lakes and pools? He fears the wind, but he fears not man, and carries on hostilities against the sun.

451. What is that huge one that controls many things and of which half faces towards Hell? It saves people's lives and grapples with the earth, if it has a trusty friend.

452. What lives in high mountains? What falls in deep valleys? What lives without breathing? What is never silent?

453. What is the marvel which I have seen outside Delling's doorway? It points its head towards Hell and turns its feet to the sun.

454. What is the marvel which I have seen outside Delling's doorway? – White fliers smiting the rock, and black fliers burying themselves in sand!

455. What is the marvel that I have seen outside Delling's doorway? This creature has ten tongues, twenty eyes, forty feet, and walks with difficulty.

456. What is the marvel which I have seen outside Delling's doorway? It flies high, with a whistling sound like the whirring of an eagle. Hard it is to clutch.

457. What is the marvel which I have seen outside Delling's doorway? It has eight feet and four eyes, and carries its knees higher than its body.

458. Who are the girls who fight without weapons around their lord? The dark red ones always protect him, and the fair ones seek to destroy him.

459. Who are the merry-maids who glide over the land for their father's pleasure? They bear a white shield in winter and a black one in summer.

460. Four walking, four hanging, two pointing the way, two warding off the dogs, one, generally dirty, dangling behind!

461. Who is that solitary one who sleeps in the grey ash, and is made from stone only? This greedy one has neither father nor mother. There will he spend his life.

462. I saw maidens like dust. Rocks were their beds. They were black and swarthy in the sunshine, but the darker it grew, the fairer they appeared.

HOLME RIDDLES, The (1650–75)
Anthology of riddles collected by the Randle Holme family of Chester.

463. who weare those that fought before the[y] were borne

464. that wch thou lookest on o traveller is a sepulcher wth out a carcasse & a carcasse wth out a sepulcher & how can that be

465. w^t is that mak[e]s tears without sorow tak[e]s his journey to heaven but dys by the way is begot wth another yet that other is not begot wth out it

466. j was round and small like a p[e]arle then long & slender as brave as an earle since like a hermit j lived in a cell & now like a rogue in the wide world j dwell

467. ther is a body w^{th}out a hart that hath a tongue & yet no head buried it was ere it was made & loud doth speek & yet is dead

468. ther is a thing no biger than a plumb that l[e]ads the king from towne to towne

469. w^t is that as lords keep in there pockets & begrs throw a way

470. though j be throwne from place to place & al unseemly as j am the nisest dame in the towne canot liue w^{th}out me

471. sisly sage sits in her kage & all her children dys for age yet she is a live & lusty

472. As j was walking late at night, j through a window chanced to spy: a gallant with his hearts delight he knew not that j was so nigh: he kissed her & close did sit to little pretty wanton Gill untill he did her favour get & likewise did obtaine his wille.

473. There is a bush fit for the nonce
That beareth pricks and precious stones
The fruit in fear some ladies pull.
Tis smooth and round and plump and full . . .
They put it in, and then they move it,
Which makes it melt, and then they love it.
So what was round, plump, full and hard
Grows lank and thin and dull and marred . . .

474. there is a thing wch hath five chins 2 hath beards 2 hath none, & one it hath but half an one.

HOMER'S RIDDLE

The riddle put to Homer by fishermen on Ios that is said to have caused his death.

475. What we caught we threw away; what we didn't catch we kept.

HOROZCO, Sebastian de (16th century)

Spanish poet. Riddles occur in *Cancionero*.

476.   *Dezidme, qual es la cosa milagrosa*
que de bocas tres alcanza,
y es en sí tan tenebrosa
y espantosa
que por todas fuego lanza?
Una boca desta alhaja come paja,
nunca bebe con ninguna;
otra tiene tal ventaja;
aunque trabaja,
que con pan se desayuna.

Aunque parece ser cosa espantosa,
y que su ser no se alcança,
quedará sin ser dudosa
ni escabrosa,
y sin ninguna dudança.

(Tell me, what is the miraculous thing which has three mouths and is so dark and dreadful that it spits fire through each of them? One mouth eats straw and never drinks, another eats bread for breakfast. Although it seems a terrible monster and its identity is hidden from view, its nature can soon be discovered and established beyond any doubt.)

477.   *Doze hijos quasi iguales*
vi á un padre que tenía
y cada qual destos tales,
legítimas, naturales
sus treynta hijas habia.
La mitad de aquestas era
de clara y blanca color,
y por contraria manera
la otra mitad saliera
de turbio y triste negror.

Y vi qu'estas hijas tales
de tal suerte procedian
que todas eran mortales,
tambien eran inmortales
segun que se sucedian.
Y trataban comunmente
con los hombres como amigas,
pero despues de repente
en el tipo mas urgente
huyan como enemigas.

(I saw a father who had twelve almost identical sons, each of which had thirty legitimate daughters. Of these, half were shining white whilst the other half were a gloomy black. And I saw that these daughters were both mortal and immortal, and though at first friendly towards men would later flee like enemies.)

ILO RIDDLE, The (n.d.)

Well-known German *Halslosungsrätsel* of folk origin.

478. On Ilo I walk, on Ilo I stand, Ilo I hold fast in my hand.

JUNIUS, Hadrian (1511–75)

German poet and emblematist. Riddles appear in *Emblematum et aenigmatum libellus* (1565).

479. *Porrigor in ramos quinos, et quilibet horum*
      Diditur in triplices nodos, nisi quintus egeret
      Uno, qui solus respondet robore cunctis,
      Undique colliculis surgo, in vallemque resido,
      Ast abaci, desit si forte, ega munia praesto.

      (I stretch out into five branches, and each of these is made into
      threefold parts, except the fifth which lacks one, and it alone
      answers to all in strength; and I rise in little hills and I sink down
      into a valley and I discharge the duties of an abacus, if by chance
      you have not got one.)

LABRAT, Dunash ben (*c.* 920–*c.* 990)

Spanish Hebrew poet from Cordova.

480. There is a box that is not full and not empty and all the boxes are
      created. It has black daughters and also reddish ones and they are
      covered with a greenish handkerchief.

481. What speaks in all languages in his riding, and his mouth spits the
      poison of life or death? It is silent when it rests, and is deaf like a
      boy or one of the poor.

482. What weeps tears without an eye, and makes everything visible
      and does not see its own garment? At the time when it approaches
      its death that which cuts off its head revives it?

LAUTERBACH, Johannes (1531–93)

Teacher in Heilbronn, Germany. Riddles published in *Aenigmata*
(1601).

483. *Sum brevis in medio, capite ac in calce diei*
      Longior, ut surgit sole caditve jubar.
      Urgentes fugio, fugientes insequor, istas
      Me videt alternis quisque subire vices.
      Defessos recreo gratas dum largior auras,
      Dumque fatigatis praebeo frigus humo.
      Nil fraudes vereor, mala nil discrimina, meque
      Sede, prior moveat se nisi, nemo movet.

(I am short in the middle, and longer at the beginning and end of the
day, as the brightness of the sun increases or declines. I flee those who
pursue me, I follow those who run away and everyone sees me
approaching those exchanges by turns. I revive the weary when I scatter

welcome breezes, and I cool those who lie exhausted on the ground. I fear no deception, no evil quarrels, and no one moves me from my seat unless he first moves himself.)

LINCOLNSHIRE HOUSEHOLD RIDDLES
A series of folk riddles submitted for publication in *Notes and Queries* (December, 1865).

484. As I was going over London Brig,
    I spies a little red thing;
    I picks it up, I sucks its blood,
    And leaves its skin to dry.

485. As I was going over Westminster Brig,
    I met a Westminster Scholar;
    He pull'd off his hat, an' drew off his glove,
    And wished me good morrow.
    Pray tell me his name, for I've told it to you.

486. As I was goin' over Humber,
    I heard a great rumble;
    Three pots a boilin',
    An' no fire under.

487. When I was going over a field of wheat,
    I picked up something good to eat,
    Neither fish, flesh, fowl nor bone,
    I kep' it till it ran alone.

488. Round the house and round the house,
    And leaves a white glove i' th' window.

489. Round the house and round the house,
    And leaves a black glove i' th' window.

490. Grows i' the wood, an' whinnies i' the moor,
    And goes up an' down our house-floor.

491. It is in the rock, but not in the stone;
    It is in the marrow, but not in the bone;
    It is in the bolster, but not in the bed;
    It is not in the living, nor yet in the dead.

LORICHIUS SECUNDUS, Johannes (d. 1569)
Lawyer to William of Orange. Also known as 'Hadamerius'. Riddles published in *Aenigmatus libris tres* (1545).

492. *Qui manibus compinget opus, non indiget illo,*
    Quique emit, hoc uti non vult, quique utitur ipso,
    Ignorat, quamvis habeat, tu solve, quid hoc sit.

(He who with his hands puts it together will not be poor, and he who buys it, does not wish to use it, and he who uses it, does not know it: now you guess what it is.)

493. *Dum juvenis fui, quattuor fontes siccavi;*
Cum autem senui, montes et valles versavi;
Post mortem meam, vivos homines ligavi.

(When I was young, I drained four springs; but when I became old, I travelled over mountains and valleys: after my death, I bound living men.)

MACAULAY, Thomas Babington (1800–59)
English historian, poet and civil servant. Riddle attributed to him.

494. Cut off my head, how singular I act!
Cut off my tail, and plural I appear!
Cut off my head and tail – most curious fact!
Although my middle's left, there's nothing there!
What is my head, cut off? A sounding sea!
What is my tail, cut off? A flowing river!
Amid their mingling depth, I fearless play,
Parent of softest sounds, though mute forever.

MAHABHARATA, THE
Hindu epic. Riddles occur in the 'Vana Parva'.

495.   *Yaksha*
What soul hath a man's which is his, yet another's?
What friend do the gods grant, the best of all others?
What joy in existence is greatest? and how
May poor men be rich and abundant? say thou.

             King
Sons are the second souls of man,
And wives the heaven-sent friends; nor can
Among all joys health be surpassed;
Contentment answereth thy last.
                    . . .
             Yaksha
Still, tell me what foeman is worst to subdue?
And what is the sickness lasts lifetime all through?
Of men that are upright, say which is the best?
And of those that are wicked, who passeth the rest?

King

Anger is man's unconquered foe;
The ache of greed doth never go;
Who loveth most of saints is first;
Of bad men cruel men are worst.

MALATESTI, Antonio (1610–*c.*1672)

Italian dramatist and poet. Riddles published in *La Sfinge* in three parts (1640, 1643, 1683).

496. *Di nulla è fatt'il Mondo, e nulla i' sono*
    E in questo nulla alfin torna ogni cosa;
    L'uom si spaventa del mio nome al suono,
    Ma s'in ch'ei non mi trova ei non ha posa.
  Tenuta bella son, brutta, o dannosa,
    Secondo ch'un è pazzo, o tristo, o buono
    Chi m'ha, d'abbandonarmi unqua non osa,
    E chi non m'ha, può darmi ad altri in dono.
  Chiamami alcun, quando il dolor l'assale;
    Ma poi vorria piuttosto altri in mia vece,
    Eppur medica son d'ogni gran male,
  Fo quel ch'i' voglio, e quel ch'i' voglio lece;
    E cotanto son giusta, e liberale
    Ch'io diedi infin me stessa a chi mi fece.

(The world is made of nothing, and I am nothing, and in the end everything returns to this nothing. Man is afraid of the sound of my name, but until he finds me cannot rest. I am held to be beautiful, ugly or injurious, according to whether one is mad, sad or good. He who has me does not dare to renounce me, and he who has not got me can give me to others. Anyone can call me when pain assails them, but then he would rather have something else in my place, and yet I am a cure for every great ill. I do what I want and I am so just and liberal that I give even myself to him who made me.)

497. *Chi vuol vedere quel che fuggir non può,*
    venga venga una volta innanzi a me,
    che s'avrà gli occhi e la ragion con sè,
    conoscerà quel ch'io gli mostrerò.
  In virtù dell'argento il tutto fo
    non avend'io religïon, nè fè;
    ignudo mostro il corpo com'egli è,
    se dal fiato dell'uom panni non ò.
  Nè m'importa, se un brutto in odio m'à,
    mentre un bello si val di mia virtù,

perchè chiara i'vo'dir la verità.
Piccola o grande vaglio meno e più;
ma se non fusse la fragilità,
varrei più, che non val tutto il Perù.

(He who wants to see what is escaping, and cannot, let him come
once first to me, for if he has got his eyes and his reason with him,
he will know what I will show him. I do everything in the virtue of
silver, having no religion or faith; I show the body, naked as it is, if
I am not clothed by the breath of man. Nor does it matter to me, if
I am held in hatred by someone ugly whilst a beautiful person
values my worth, because I will speak the truth clearly. The small
or the large I consider less and more; and if it were not for my
fragility, I would be worth more than the whole of Peru.)

MEGALOMITES, Basilios (11th century)
Byzantine poet contemporary with Michael Psellus.

498. There is such a male as the one who came out of a white stone; at
a distance his beard sparkles like flame; the earth trembles under
his feet; when he cries out, the devils run for shelter; a gust of
wind comes from under his wings.

MENESTRIER, Claude François (1631–1705)
French Jesuit historian and heraldic scholar. Riddles appear in *La
philosophie des images énigmatiques* (1694).

499. *Je suis de divers lieux, je nais dans les Forêts,*
    Tantôt près des ruisseaux, tantôt près des marais,
    Je suis de toute taille & de seche figure,
    Je n'ai jambes ni bras, cependant la nature
    Ne m'a pas fait un monstre, & j'en vaux beaucoup mieux,
    Reparant ce deffaut par un grand nombre d'yeux;
    Qu'ils soient toûjours ouverts, il n'est pas necessaire,
    Qu'ils soient fermez ou non, ils sçavent toûjours plaire.
    Comme un Cameleon je me nourris de l'air.
    Quoi que je ne puisse parler
    J'ai le don de me faire entendre
    Et par une vertu qui pourra vous surprendre
    Ce qu'en ouvrant la bouche on voit faire en tous lieux
    A mille gens qui par là savent plaire,
    Moi de qui la methode à la leur est contraire
    Je le fais en fermant la plûpart de mes yeux.

(I come from various places: I was born in the forest, sometimes
near streams, sometimes near marshes. I can be of any size and
have a dry body. I have neither legs nor arms, but nature hasn't

made me a monster, and I am worth much more than that, compensating for this defect by giving me a great many eyes. It is not necessary for them always to be open – open or shut they always know how to please. Like a chameleon I live on air. Though I cannot speak I have the gift of making people listen to me, and in a manner that would surprise you: instead of opening my mouth – by which a thousand folk know how to please – I, whose method is the opposite, do so by shutting most of my eyes.)

500. *Avec une tête assez grosse*
D'un pied je me tiens sans effort.
Bien que petit de taille, & rien moins qu'un Colosse
J'ai quelquefois terrassé le plus fort.
Quoi que je sois dans l'impuissance
De faire un seul pas pour marcher,
Je viens pourtant toûjours en grande diligence;
Mais qui me veut peut me venir chercher.
De tels dons j'étois les delices
Et qui m'avoient ouvert leur coeur
Je n'ai que trop souvent fait de grands sacrifices
Pour m'avoir pris dans ma mauvaise humeur.
Chercher, tâchez de me comprendre;
Mais quand vous m'aurez deviné
A mes freres bâtards gardez de vous meprendre,
C'est un coup seur d'en être assassiné.

(With quite a big head I stand easily on one foot. Although I am small, and anything but a Colossus, I have been known to knock down the strongest. Though I am unable to walk a single step, I still keep turning up each day with great speed; but anyone who wants me must come and find me. For those to whom I am a delicacy and who open their hearts to me I have only too often made great sacrifices for having taken me when I was in a bad mood. Now look and try to find me out; but when you have guessed my meaning make sure you do not mistake me for my bastard brothers, for this is certain death.)

501. *Inconstante & legere*
Je me fais aimer constamment,
Et le plus agréable Amant
Sans moi ne sçauroit plaire.
   Fille de Roturier,
Des plus nobles Galans je reçois les hommages,
Je cede aux fous, & je command aux sages,
Je ne fais rien & suis de tout métier,
La raison contre moi n'est jamais la plus forte,

Le Roy même a souvent reconnu mon pouvoir.
Je decide à la Cour de tout sans rien savoir,
Et malgré les Sçavans mon suffrage l'emporte.
  On ne sçauroit compter mes ans.
    Mon extreme vieillesse
      Egale celle du tems,
Je plais pourtant par ma jeunesse.

(Fickle and flighty I constantly make myself loved and even the most charming suitor could not succeed without me. Daughter of a commoner, I receive tribute from the noblest gallants; I suffer fools gladly yet I rule wise men; I do nothing and yet am a member of every profession; reason will never win against me, even the king himself has often admitted my power. I decide everything at court without knowing anything, and, in spite of the scholars, it's my word that counts. No one could tell how old I am. My great age is the age of time itself, but even so I charm with my youthfulness.)

502. *On ne voit point dans la nature*
   De corps plus petit que le mien,
   Et cependant je fais si bien
   Que je suis plus fecond qu'aucune creature
   J'aurois trop de fureur dans les grandes chaleurs,
   L'hiver est destiné pour me metre en usage,
   J'ai l'humeur si piquante, & l'esprit si sauvage
   Que plus on me cherit, plus on verse de pleurs.
   Pour se servir de moi qu'on me mette en poussiere,
   Qu'on emploïe à me batre & la nuit & le jour
   Je n'en serai pas moins audacieuse & fiere,
   Malheur aux gens qui me font trop de cour.

(You'll never see anything in the whole of Nature with a body smaller than mine, yet I am so good at creating things that I am more fertile than any other creature. I would be too fiery in the hot season, winter is the best time to put me to use. My disposition is so sharp, and my spirit so wild that the more I am cherished, the more I cause tears. He who would employ me must first render me to dust, and beat me both night and day. But still I shall be not less audacious and proud, woe betide those who court me too much.)

MERCURE DE FRANCE, LE (1672–1965)
French fortnightly review which included enigmas, logographs and charades up to 1810.

503. *Je brille avec six pieds, avec cinq je te couvre.*

504. *Par quatre pieds j'entends, et par trois je réponds.*

505. *Pour lier avec moi longue société,*
   Un habitant d'un rivage écarté
   A traversé des mers l'espace formidable;
   Et tandis que, brûlant d'une âme durable,
   Il périt dans mon sein, de ses feux tourmenté,
   De qui nous réunit il fait la volupté.
   C'est du même élément le pouvoir redoutable
   Qui me donne, qui m'ôte et me rend ma beauté.
      Quand une fois j'ai la tête allumée,
   Je fais à mes amis une grande leçon.
   Philosophe muet, je prêche à ma façon
      Que tout ici n'est que fumée.

(To bind itself in long companionship with me, a resident of a far-flung shore has crossed the vast space of the seas; and whilst burning with a lasting flame it slowly dies in my breast tormented by its own fires, it gives pleasure to the one who joins us. It is the formidable power of this same ingredient that gives, takes away and gives me back my beauty. Once my head is set alight I give my friends a great lesson. A dumb philosopher, in my own way I preach that there is nothing here but smoke.)

506. *Avec six pieds, je suis un mets fort restaurant;*
   Avec cinq, des traités je deviens le garant;
   Avec quatre, mes flots roulent avec vitesse;
   Avec trois, en fuyant j'emporte la jeunesse.

(With six feet, I am a very fortifying dish; with five, I become the guarantee of the treaty; with four, my waters run swift; with three, in fleeing I steal away youth.)

507. *Nous sommes quatre enfants d'une grande famille,*
   Et nous avons deux espèces de sœurs.
   A notre tête est la troisième fille,
   Et notre aînée a les seconds honneurs.
   Celle qui de nous quatre a la taille plus grande,
   A la troisième place a soumis sa fierté,
   Et par distinction la dernière demande
      Un petit ornement sur son chef ajouté.
      Nous composons un tout; mettez-vous à sa quête,
      Et si vous le trouvez, demandez-le d'abord
         Pour vous guérir du mal de tête
      Que vous aura causé peut-être cet effort.

(We are four children of a big family, and we have two kinds of sister. At our head is the third daughter, and the eldest has second place. She who is the tallest of us four has condescended to take the third place, and in order to be noticed the last asks for a small ornament on her head. Together we form a single whole; go and search for the solution and if you find it, ask at once for some of it to cure the headache that this effort may have given you.)

508. *De filer le produit de ma riche semence,*
Le secret, par Isis, aux mortels fut donné;
Je naquis, dit l'histoire, aux bords d'un fleuve immense,
Dont le nom mémorable est mon nom retourné.

(The secret of spinning the product of my rich seed was given to mortals by Isis. I was born, says history, on the banks of a vast river, whose memorable name is my name back to front.)

MIRTUNZIO, Fosildo (18th century)

Pseudonymous Italian riddler. Enigmas published in *Veglie autunnali* (1796).

509. *Forrier di pace, e di tranquilla quiete,*
Dopo tempeste strepitose, e dense,
Tu mi vedi apparir su d'alte mete
Pinto in vario color, che mi condense,
Mi dileguo in brev'or per vie secrete,
Incapibili omai, perchè già immense:
Mi tinge un Astro, ed al sparir di quello,
Finisco anch'io, e in questo dir mi svello.

(Portender of peace, and of quiet tranquillity, after loud, large storms, you see me appear on high, painted in various colours which condense me, I fade away shortly by secret paths, no longer understandable, because already vast. A star paints me, and when it disappears, I too finish, and in saying this I reveal myself.)

510. *Ancella fida son di notte, e giorno,*
Compagna indivisibil sempre a lato;
Moto, e gesto non fai, che già d'intorno
Gli rassomiglio oscura per usato;
Con te già vivo, e faccio il mio soggiorno,
Nè posso mai cambiar si nobil stato,
Perchè mi scorta in te luce diurna
E mi guida talor face notturna.

(I am a faithful maid by night and by day, an inseparable companion always by your side. You make no movement or gesture, without my being there looking like you, but obscured as usual. I already live with you, and I make my sojourn with you, nor can I ever change such a noble state, because daily light makes me follow you, and sometimes even the face of night guides me.)

MOTHER GOOSE'S TALES (*c.* 1729)

Translation by Samber of Perrault's children's anthology *Contes de ma mère l'Oye* (1697) containing riddle-rhymes.

511. Black I am and much admired,
     Men seek me until they're tired;
     When they find me, break my head,
     And take me from my resting bed.

512. A house full, a hole full,
     And you cannot gather a bowl full.

513. Highty tighty, paradighty,
     Clothed all in green,
     The king could not read it,
     No more could the queen;
     They sent for the wise men
     From out of the East,
     Who said it had horns,
     But it was not a beast.

514. I'm called by the name of a man,
     Yet am as little as a mouse;
     When winter comes I love to be
     With my red target near the house.

515. Two brothers we are,
     Great burdens we bear,
     On which we are bitterly pressed;
     The truth is to say,
     We are full all the day,
     And empty when we go to rest.

516. Clothed in yellow, red, and green,
     I prate before the king and queen;
     Of neither house nor land possessed,
     By lords and knights I am caressed.

517. Little Nancy Etticoat
     In a white petticoat
     And a red nose;
     The longer she stands
     The shorter she grows.

518. In spring I am gay,
     In handsome array;
     In summer more clothing I wear;
     When colder it grows,
     I fling off my clothes;
     And in winter quite naked appear.

519. I have a little sister called Peep, Peep, Peep,
   She wades in the water deep, deep, deep.
   She climbs the mountain high, high, high,
   My poor little sister has but one eye.

520. Old Mother Twitchett had but one eye,
   And a long tail which she let fly;
   And every time she went over a gap,
   She left a bit of her tail in a trap.

521. Little Billy Breek
   Sits by the reek
   He has more horns
   Than all the king's sheep.

522. Thirty white horses upon a red hill,
   Now they champ, now they clamp,
   And now they stand still.

523. As I was going over London Bridge,
   I heard something crack;
   Not a man in all England
   Can mend that!

524. Flour of England, fruit of Spain,
   Met together in a shower of rain;
   Put in a bag, tied round with string.
   If you tell me this riddle
   I'll give you a ring.

NEW RIDDLE BOOK FOR THE AMUSEMENT AND INSTRUCTION OF LITTLE MISSES AND MASTERS, The (19th century)

Chapbook by 'Master Wiseman', printed by James Kendrew of York.

525. I'm a busy active creature,
   Full of mirth and play by nature;
   Nimbly I skip from tree to tree,
   To get the food that's fit for me;
   Then let me hear if you can tell,
   What is my name, and where I dwell.

526. I'm captain of a party small,
   Whose number is but five,
   But yet do great exploits for all,
   And ev'ry man alive.
   With Adam I was seen to live,
   Ere he knew what was evil;
   But no connection have with Eve,

The serpent, or the devil.
I on our Saviour's law attend,
    And fly deceit and vice;
Patriot and Protestant befriend,
    But Infidels despise.

527. Midst numbers round I spy'd a beauty fair,
More charming than her sisters were:
With blushing cheek she tempting of me stood,
At last I cropt her bloom and suck'd her blood,
Sweet meat she was, but neither flesh nor bone,
Yet in her tender heart she had a stone.

528. Four wings I have, and sometimes more,
    By which I move and fly;
Yet never stir until I'm drove,
    So indolent am I.

529. I daily am in France and Spain,
At times do all the world explore,
Since time I've held my reign,
And shall till time will be no more.
I never in my life beheld,
A garden, field, or river clear;
Yet neither garden, spring, or field,
Can flourish if I am not there.

530.   My body is thin,
    And has no guts within,
I have neither head, face, nor eye;
    But a tail I have got,
    As long as – what not,
And without any wings I can fly.

PANARCES (n.d.)

Ancient Greek poet, cited by Athenaeus in *Deipnosophistae*. A version of the riddle is also mentioned by Plato in *Republic*, Book V.

531. A man that was not a man hit a bird that was not a bird, perched on wood that was not wood, with a stone that was not stone.

PASSOVER RIDDLE, The (n.d.)

Ancient riddle recited at Jewish Passover Eve celebrations.

532. Who knoweth one? I (saith Israel) know One:
    One is God, who is over heaven and earth.
Who knoweth two? I (saith Israel) know two:

Two tables of the covenant; but One is our God
Who is over the heavens and the earth.

[And so on to the last verse, which is:

Who knoweth thirteen? I (saith Israel) know thirteen: Thirteen
divine attributes, twelve tribes, eleven stars, ten commandments,
nine months preceding childbirth, eight days preceding
circumcision, seven days of the week, six books of the Mishnah,
five books of the Law, four matrons, three patriarchs, two tables of
the covenant; but One is our God who is over the heavens and the
earth.]

PETER PRIMROSE'S BOOKS FOR BOYS AND GIRLS: RIDDLES (*c.* 1850)

Chapbook printed by William Walker of Oxley, Yorkshire.

533. Many a lady in the land
Has grasp'd me in her lily hand;
I'm sometimes made a little bright,
And often us'd to make more light.

534. To cross the water I'm the way,
For water I'm above:
I touch it not, and, truth to say,
I neither swim nor move.

535. Horns tho' I wear, in yonder sky
Astronomers have plac'd me high;
The seeds of cruelty I nourish,
And 'mongst Hibernia's children flourish.

536. My tongue is long,
My voice is strong,
And yet I breed no strife;
You will me hear,
Both far and near,
And yet I have no life.

537. My first does innocence express;
My second, 'tis a part of dress:
United, they a period show
That's free from vices, guilt and woe.

538. I live in a study, but know not a letter;
I feast on the muses but am ne'er the better:
Can run over English, o'er Latin, o'er Greek,
But none of the languages ever could speak.

539. I am the beginning of sorrow, and the end of sickness. You cannot
express happiness without me; yet I am in the midst of crosses. I
am always in risk, yet never in danger. You may find me in the
sun, but I am never out of darkness.

540. I at fires attend,
Am a kitchen friend;
When my nose I blow,
How the embers glow!
When the wind compels,
How my belly swells!

POE, Edgar Allan (1809–49)

American poet and story-writer. Riddles and acrostics appeared in
various literary magazines. (To translate the first two, read the first
letter of the first line in connection with the second letter of the second
line, the third letter of the third line, the fourth of the fourth, and so on
to the end. The names will thus appear. To solve the third riddle, take
the first letter of the name of each writer described in the text – together
they also form a word.)

541. For her this rhyme is penned, whose luminous eyes,
Brightly expressive as the twins of Læda,
Shall find her own sweet name, that, nestling lies
Upon the page, enwrapped from every reader.
Search narrowly the lines! – they hold a treasure
Divine – a talisman – an amulet.
That must be worn *at heart*. Search well the measure –
The words – the syllables! Do not forget
The trivialest point, or you may lose your labour!
And yet there is in this no Gordian knot
Which one might not undo without a sabre,
If one could merely comprehend the plot.
Enwritten upon the leaf where now are peering
Eyes scintillating soul, there lie *perdus*
Three eloquent words oft uttered in the hearing
Of poets, by poets – as the name is a poet's, too.
Its letters, although naturally lying
Like the knight Pinto – Mendez Ferdinando –
Still form a synonym for Truth. – Cease trying!
You will not read the riddle, though you do the best you *can* do.

542. 'Seldom we find,' says Solomon Don Dunce,
'Half an idea in the profoundest sonnet.
Through all the flimsy things we see at once
As easily as through a Naples bonnet –

Trash of all trash! – how *can* a lady don it?
Yet heavier far than your Petrarchan stuff –
Owl-downy nonsense that the faintest puff
    Twirls into trunk-paper the while you con it.'
And, veritably, Sol is right enough.
The general tuckermanities are arrant
Bubbles – ephemeral and *so* transparent –
    But *this* is, now, – you may depend upon it –
Stable, opaque, immortal – all by dint
Of the dear names that lie concealed within 't.

543. The noblest name in Allegory's page,
    The hand that traced inexorable rage;
    A pleasing moralist whose page refined,
    Displays the deepest knowledge of the mind;
    A tender poet of a foreign tongue,
    (Indited in the language that he sung).
    A bard of brilliant but unlicensed page
    At once the shame and glory of our age,
    The prince of harmony and stirling sense,
    The ancient dramatist of eminence,
    The bard that paints imagination's powers,
    And him whose song revives departed hours,
    Once more an ancient tragic bard recall,
    In boldness of design surpassing all.
    These names when rightly read, a name [make] known
    Which gathers all their glories in its own.

PSELLUS, Michael (*fl.* 1075–1100)
Greek encyclopedist and diplomat.

544. I am justice. I am the height of justice. I have six ribs, but only two
    legs.

PUCCINI, Giacomo (1858–1924)
Italian opera composer. Riddles contained in Act 2 of *Turandot* (1926),
based on plays by Gozzi and Schiller (libretto by G. Adami and R.
Simoni).

545. In the dark night flies a many-hued phantom.
    It soars and spreads its wings
    above the gloomy human crowd.
    The whole world calls to it,
    the whole world implores it.
    At dawn the phantom vanishes
    to be reborn in every heart.

And every night 't is born anew
and every day it dies!

546. It kindles like a flame
but it is not flame.
At times it is a frenzy.
It is fever, force, passion!
Inertia makes it flag.
If you lose heart or die it grows cold,
but dream of conquest and it flares up.
Its voice you heed in trepidation,
it glows like the setting sun!

547. Ice which gives you fire
and which your fire
freezes still more!
Lily-white and dark,
if it allows you your freedom
it makes you a slave;
if it accepts you as a slave
it makes you a King!

PUNCH, or The London Charivari (1841–date)
English illustrated weekly comic periodical. Conundrums taken from an issue of 1843.

548. Why are washerwomen the greatest navigators of the globe?

549. Why is 'Yes' the most ignorant word in the language?

550. Why is a railroad like a bug?

551. Why is a man who has too many servants like an oyster?

552. Why is a rook's throat like a road?

553. Why is a cornfield gayer than any other?

554. Why is a cow's tail like a swan's bosom?

555. Why is a pig in a parlour like a house on fire?

556. Why is the sun like a good loaf?

557. Why is a bird a greedy creature?

558. When is a fowl's neck like a bell?

559. Why isn't a boy like a pretty bonnet?

560. When is a lady like a trout?

PUTTENHAM, Richard (1520–1601)

English author and critic. Riddles occur in *The Arte of English Poesie* (1589).

561. It is my mother well I wot
And yet the daughter that I begot.

562. I haue a thing and rough it is
And in the midst a hole I wis:
There came a yong man with his ginne,
And he put it a handfull in.

PUZZLE BOOK, The (*c.* 1820)

Chapbook printed by William Davison of Alnwick (1781–1858).

563. I timely go to rest at night,
    And with the sun I rise;
All day I try to reach in flight,
    That place where no one dies.

564. Old Mother old stands in the cold,
Her children die with age:
Yet she still lives, and brings forth young,
And every one without a tongue.

565. I daily view the world around,
And in one place I'm seldom found;
I never eat, yet by my power,
Procure what millions do devour.

566. My virtue is such, that I
Can do the things with ease,
Which strength and force will never do,
Employ them as you please.

567. Tho' I both foul and dirty am,
    As black as black as can be,
There's many a Lady that will come,
    And by the hand take me.

568. We dwell in cottages of straw,
And labour much for little gains;
Sweet meat from us our masters draw,
And then with death reward our pains.

569. Tho' I have neither legs nor feet,
    My use is for to go;
Altho' I cannot speak, I tell
    What others want to know.

QUEEN OF SHEBA'S RIDDLES, The (n.d.)

Riddles later ascribed to the Queen of Sheba (apocryphal).

570. Seven there are that issue and nine that enter;
Two yield the draught and one drinks.

571. There is an enclosure with ten doors;
When one is open, nine are shut;
When nine are open, one is shut.

572. A woman said to her son,
'Thy father is my father,
And thy grandfather my husband;
Thou art my son, and I am thy sister.'

RABELAIS, François (1494–1553)

French humanist, satirist and physician. Riddles occur in *Pantagruel*
(1532), *Gargantua* (1534) and the 'Fifth Book' (1562–4) from which this
example is taken.

573. A pretty creature, young and fair and slender,
Conceived, without a sire, a swarthy son
And bore him painlessly, the little tender
Suckling, although his birth was a strange one.
For, like a viper, through her side he bored
Impatiently, a truly hideous thing,
And then o'er hill and valley boldly soared,
Riding the air, or o'er land journeying;
Which drove the Friend of Wisdom out of his mind,
For he had thought him of the human kind.

RECEUIL DES ÉNIGMES DE CES TEMPS (1659)

French riddle collection edited by Abbé C. Cotin.

574. *De mille ouvriers i'occupe le loisir,*
Ie porte un masque au visage semblable,
Qui me cachant, irrite le desir,
Car au grand iour ie suis moins agreable.

Souvent i'eschappe à qui me croit saisir,
Et les beaux traits qui me rendent aymable
Font de la peine, & causent du plaisir,
Mais trop de fard me rend reconnoissable.

En plein midy mon sçavoir nompareil,
Peut mettre un voile au devant du Soleil.
Vous qui percez l'obscurité plus forte.

Ie vous invite à démesler ce poinct,

Qui me connoist m'appelle en mesme sorte,
Que l'ignorant qui ne me connoist point.

(I occupy the leisure of a thousand workers. I wear a mask like a face which, hiding me, inflames desire, for I am less attractive in broad daylight. I often escape those who think they can catch me, and the good features that make me lovable are both sources of pain, and yet also cause pleasure. But too much make-up makes me recognizable. At high noon my unparalleled knowledge can even put a veil in front of the sun. You, who can pierce a stronger darkness, I ask you to untangle this puzzle. He who knows me calls me by the same name as the ignoramus who doesn't know me at all.)

575. *Mon pere n'est qu'esprit, & gouverne la terre,*
Son estre est immortel, il est fait pour les Cieux,
Il me produit obscure, & reserve à ses yeux
L'honneur de penetrer le voille qui m'enserre,
Dans une sombre nuict ie cache mes tresors,
Ie fais ce que ie puis, de peur d'estre apperceuë,
Mais dedans ce dessein souvent ie suis deceuë,
Un seul mot me confond, & descouvre mon corps.

(My father is just a spirit, and he governs the earth. His being is immortal, he is made for the heavens. He makes me obscure and keeps for his own eyes the honour of piercing the veil which encloses me. In a dark night I conceal my treasures. I do whatever I can, for fear of discovery, but I am often disappointed in my purpose. A single word confounds me and exposes me.)

REUSNER, Nicolaus (1545–1602)

Rector of Jena University, Germany. Riddles published in *Aenigmata* (1602). Also edited an anthology, *Aenigmatographia*.

576. *Foemina, piscis, avis sum, nautas fallere docta,*
Sum scopulus, non sum foemina, piscis, avis.

(I am a woman, a fish and a bird, well taught to deceive sailors. I am a rock, I am not a woman, or a fish or a bird.)

577. *Sunt gemina germana, harum alteram et altera gignit,*
Perque vices sic fit, filia nata, parens.

(They are twin sisters; each of them gives birth to the other, and thus it happens that, by turns, a daughter is born, then a parent.)

578. *Lacryma multa mihi, sed nulla est causa doloris,*
Coeli affecto vitam, sed gravis aer obest.

(Many are the tears I give but there is no cause for grief. I strive for life in the sky, but the weighty air engulfs me.)

RIDDLE BALLADS, English (18th century)

Some slightly abridged texts of famous English riddle ballads.

579.   'A Noble Riddle Wisely Expounded'

> There was a lady of the North Country,
>   Lay the bent to the bonny broom
> And she had lovely daughters three.
>   Fa la la la, fa la la la ra re
>
> There was a knight of noble worth
> Which also lived in the North.
>
> The knight, of courage stout and brave,
> A wife he did desire to have.
>
> He knocked at the ladie's gate
> One evening when it was late.
>
> The eldest sister let him in,
> And pin'd the door with a silver pin.
>
> The second sister she made his bed,
> And laid soft pillows under his head.
>
> The youngest daughter that same night,
> She went to bed to this young knight.
>
> And in the morning, when it was day,
> These words unto him she did say:
>
> 'Now you have had your will,' quoth she,
> 'I pray, sir knight, will you marry me?'
>
> The young brave knight to her replyed,
> 'Thy suit, fair maid, shall not be deny'd.
>
> 'If thou canst answer me questions three,
> This very day will I marry thee.'
>
> 'Kind sir, in love, O then,' quoth she,
> 'Tell me what your [three] questions be.'
>
> 'O what is longer than the way,
> Or what is deeper than the sea?
>
> 'Or what is louder than the horn,
> Or what is sharper than a thorn?
>
> 'Or what is greener than the grass,
> Or what is worse than a woman was?'
>
> 'O love is longer than the way,
> And hell is deeper than the sea.
>
> 'And thunder is louder than the horn,
> And hunger is sharper than a thorn.

'And poyson is greener than the grass,
And the Devil is worse than woman was.'

When she these questions answered had,
The knight became exceeding glad.

And having [truly] try'd her wit,
He much commended her for it.

And after, as it is verifi'd,
He made of her his lovely bride.

So now, fair maidens all, adieu,
This song I dedicate to you.

I wish that you may constant prove
Unto the man that you do love.

580.   'Captain Wedderburn's Courtship'

The Lord of Rosslyn's daughter gaed through the
     wud her lane,
And there she met Captain Wedderburn, a servant
     to the king.
He said unto his livery-man, Were 't na agen the
     law,
I wad tak her to my ain bed, and lay her at the wa.
                    . . .
Then he lap aff his milk-white steed, and set the lady
     on,
And a' the way he walkd on foot, he held her by the
     hand;
He held her by the middle jimp, for fear that she
     should fa;
Saying, I'll tak ye to my ain bed, and lay thee at the
     wa.
                    . . .
'O haud awa frae me, kind sir, I pray ye lat me be,
For I'll na lie in your bed till I get dishes three;
Dishes three maun be dressd for me, gif I should eat
     them a',
Before I lie in your bed, at either stock or wa.

''T is I maun hae to my supper a chicken without a
     bane;
And I maun hae to my supper a cherry without a
     stane;
And I maun hae to my supper a bird without a gaw,
Before I lie in your bed, at either stock or wa.'

'Whan the chicken's in the shell, I am sure it has na
  bane;
And whan the cherry's in the bloom, I wat it has na
  stane;
The dove she is a genty bird, she flees without a
  gaw;
Sae we'll baith lie in ae bed, and ye'll be at the wa.'

    . . .

'O haud awa frae me, kind sir, I pray don't me
  perplex,
For I'll na lie in your bed till ye answer questions six:
Questions six ye maun answer me, and that is four
  and twa,
Before I lie in your bed, at either stock or wa.

'O what is greener than the gress, what's higher
  than thae trees?
O what is worse than women's wish, what's deeper
  than the seas?
What bird craws first, what tree buds first, what
  first does on them fa?
Before I lie in your bed, at either stock or wa.'

'Death is greener than the gress, heaven higher than
  thae trees;
The devil's waur than women's wish, hell's deeper
  than the seas;
The cock craws first, the cedar buds first, dew first
  on them does fa;
Sae we'll baith lie in ae bed, and ye 'se lie at the wa.'

Little did this lady think, that morning when she
  raise,
That this was for to be the last o a' her maiden days.
But there's na into the king's realm to be found a
  blither twa,
And now she's Mrs. Wedderburn, and she lies at the
  wa.

'T was on a night, an evening bright,
   When the dew began to fa,
Lady Margaret was walking up and down,
   Looking oer her castle wa.

She looked east and she looked west,
   To see what she could spy,
When a gallant knight came in her sight,
   And to the gate drew nigh.

'You seem to be no gentleman,
   You wear your boots so wide;
But you seem to be some cunning hunter,
   You wear the horn so syde.'

'I am no cunning hunter,' he said,
   'Nor neer intend to be;
But I am come to this castle
   To seek the love of thee.
And if you do not grant me love,
   This night for thee I'll die.'

'If you should die for me, sir knight,
   There's few for you will meane;
For mony a better has died for me,
   Whose graves are growing green.

'But ye maun read my riddle,' she said,
   'And answer my questions three;
And but ye read them right,' she said,
   'Gae stretch ye out and die.

'Now what is the flower, the ae first flower,
   Springs either on moor or dale?
And what is the bird, the bonnie bonnie bird,
   Sings on the evening gale?'

'The primrose is the ae first flower
   Springs either on moor or dale,
And the thristlecock is the bonniest bird
   Sings on the evening gale.'

. . .

'I think you maun be my match,' she said,
   'My match and something mair;
You are the first eer got the grant
   Of love frae my father's heir.'

RIDDLE BALLADS, Faroese

Abridged text of Ancient Faroese ballad, *Gátu Ríma*.

582. Guest goes wandering from the hall,
    Silent and blind is he;
  Meets he with an eldern man
    All with hair so grey.

Meets he with an eldern man,
    All with hair so grey;
'Why art thou so silent, Guest the Blind,
    And wherefore dost thou stray?'

'It is not so wonderful
    Though I of speech am slow;
For riddles have brought me to an evil pass,
    And I lose my head tomorrow.'

    . . .

'How much of the red, red gold
    Wilt thou give to me,
If I go in before King Heithrek
    And ask thy riddles for thee?'

'Twelve marks of the red, red gold
    Will I give to thee,
If thou wilt go in before King Heithrek,
    And ransom my head for me.'

'Go thou into thy courtyard
    And look to thy dwelling, thou,
While I go in before King Heithrek,
    And ask him riddles now.'

    . . .

'O hearken now, Heithrek my King,
    And what can this be now? –
Soft as down and hard as horn,
    And white as glistening snow!'

'Hear thou this now, Guest the Blind;
    This riddle I understand. –
The sea it is both soft and hard,
    And flings white spray upon the land.'

'O hearken now, Heithrek my King,
    Where does the sapling grow, –
Its root is turned towards high Heaven,
    And its head turned down below?'

'The icicle on the high crags,
   No sapling it is I trow,
Yet its root is turned towards high heaven,
   And its head turned down below.'

'O hearken now, Heithrek my King,
   Where does that forest grow, –
It is cut on every holy day,
   And yet there is wood enow?'

'The beard which grows on each man's chin,
   No forest is that I trow,
Though shaved on every holy day,
   And yet there is wood enow.'

'O hearken now, Heithrek my King,
   Where dost thou know the brothers, –
Both of them live in the same hall,
   And have neither fathers nor mothers?'

'Turf clods and brimstones,
   Neither of the twain are brothers.
Both of them live in the same hall,
   And have neither fathers nor mothers.'

· · . . .

Othin has turned into a wild fowl,
   And has flown far out to sea;
He has burnt King Heithrek in his hall,
   And all his company.

RIDDLE OF THE SPHINX, The

Traditional Greek riddle. Mentioned in Athenaeus's *Deipnosophistae* but also occurs in *Greek Anthology* and elsewhere.

583. What is it that goes on four legs in the morning, two legs at noon and three legs in the evening?

RIDDLES, CHARADES, AND CONUNDRUMS (1822)

584. What is that which a coach always goes with, cannot go without, and yet is of no use to the coach?

585. What is put on a table, cut, but never eaten?

586. What has three feet and cannot walk?

RIDDLES OF HERACLITUS AND DEMOCRITUS (1598)

Anonymous riddle collection printed in London.

587. Many a man doth speake of mee,
     But no man ever shall me see,
     For all in one doe full agree
     That no where must my dwelling bee.

588. I wrinkled am and passing olde,
     But gallant is my motion,
     Abhorring aie to be controulde
     By any ones devotion.
     Come all that list on me to mount,
     Sure I will not forsake them,
     But let them make their just account,
     That finely I shall shake them.
     Ne doe I aske men ought for hose,
     For shooes, for drinke, or meating,
     Come all that list with me to close
     Sans paying or intreating.
     And they may chaunce finde in my wombe
     To make them wish they were at home.

589. A female, produced first in a rude lumpe, as they say a yong beare
     is, not by licking, but by pressing became beautifull. For she hath
     as many friendes as the Queene of England, as many subjectes as
     the King of Spaine, as many rulers as Athens ever had, or Venice
     hath. And though shee can neither write nor reade, yet is she
     lettered, a phisition, a rhetorician, and a chronicler.

590. We are in number not five times five,
     No one of us two handfull long,
     Nor any of us takes care to thrive,
     Yet all together we doe so throng,
     That if a man would lift to strive
     T'extinguish or to doe us wrong,
     Were he the greatest prince alive,
     We should be found for him too strong,
     And could make him infamous in time to come,
     Though most of us beene deafe and dombe.

591. This is the age that I would have,
     These times for me are woondrous fit;
     Each ladie that is fine and brave
     With me delights to goe and sit.
     My living lieth not in my lands,
     Yet I am daintie, fine and sweete.

The ladies take me in their hands,
    Their lips and mine full often meete.
Their paps, their cheekes I well may touch,
    In smiling sort with me they play,
Their husbands thereat thinke not much,
    No, though I downe with them doe lay:
In sooth, it is a foolish sin,
When foolish husbands iealous bin.

592. Two forward went, and one did seeme to stay them;
Foure after ran, and five did overlay them,
Of which one dead foure quicke was comprehending:
And all these twelve unto one marke were tending.

593. First I was small, and round like a pearle;
Then long and slender, as brave as an earle;
Since, like an hermit, I livde in a cell,
And now, like a rogue, in the wide world I dwell.

594. There is a bodie without a hart, that hath a toong, and yet no head;
Buried it was, ere it was made, and lowde it speakes, and yet is
dead.

595. A lowe bred squire,
Borne in the mire,
That never knew who was his sire,

Being armed light,
After midnight
(No remedie) would needes go fight.

In corslet bad
The youth was clad,
And sarcenet sleeves for sooth he had.

But at a word:
He had no sword,
Nor other weapon woorth a *etc* [*sic*].

Ne was he strong,
Nor large nor long,
But foorth he came with a hideous song.

And Tartar leeke
He me did seeke,
Lighting at first full on my cheeke.

This thing of naught
At face still raught,
As Cesar once his souldiours taught,

When they should fight

Against that knight,
Pompey defending countries right:

So in like case
This varlet base
Was ever poring at my face.

I could not rest
Within my nest,
The rascall did me so molest.

I had the Jacke
Soone brought to wracke,
Had he not ever retired backe.

But he comes, he goes,
He fell, he rose,
He bit me by the very nose.

It made me sweare,
And God to teare,
I could not for my life forbeare.

That such a knave
Should be so brave,
Would make (I trowe) a saint to rave.

But clod or stone,
Or sticke or bone,
Or gunne or crosbowe had I none.

That, truth to showe,
I did not knowe,
Which way I might him overthrowe.

So that at last
I waxt agast,
And, longing t'have the combate past,

I hid my head
Within a bed
And slept like one that had been dead.

596. Mounsier Monoculus, with that one eie,
It's not for his personage or his sweete face,
That wherefoere I goe, I doe him espie,
    With maidens and wives in speciall grace.
He is a surgeon, he can let blood,
His pricke is a thing that doth them good.

597. That which a sheepe did inward hide,
I use to weare on my outside;

166

And that which a tree did outward weare,
    Within me alwaies I doe beare.
By drowning first I tooke effence,
    And hanged was since for none offence:
Still ready, by a blast of breath,
To finde a life causing my death.

598. Al day leeke one that's in disgrace
    He resteth in some secret place,
And seldome putteth foorth the head,
    Untill daylight be fully fled;
Then in the maides or goodwives hand
    The gallant ginnes first up to stand:
Whom to a hole they doe apply,
Wherein he will both live and die.

RIG-VEDA, The (*c.* 1000 BC)
Hindu religious text.

599. The one who made him does not know him. He escapes from the one who has seen him. Enveloped in his mother's womb, he is subject to annihilation, while he has many descendants.

600. Breathing, it lies there and is nevertheless quick in its gait, moving and yet fixed in the rivers. The soul of the dead man goes about as it likes. The immortal one has the same origin as the mortal one.

601. I saw a restless shepherd travelling back and forth on his paths. He garbs himself in that which goes in the same and in an opposite direction. He goes hither and thither among creatures.

602. The wheel of nature with twelve spokes turns around the heavens without ever going to ruin. On it stand, O Agni, sons in pairs to the number of seven hundred and twenty.

ROUSSEAU, Jean Jacques (1712–78)
French political philosopher and educationalist. Riddle published in 1776.

603. *Enfant de l'Art, Enfant de la Nature,*
    Sans prolonger les jours j'empêche de mourir:
    Plus je suis vrai, plus je fais d'imposture,
    Et je deviens trop jeune à force de vieillir.

(Child of Art, Child of Nature, without prolonging life, I prevent death: the truer I am, the more false I appear, and I become too young as age creeps on.)

ROYAL RIDDLE BOOK, The (1820)

604. In the bed it stands, in the bed it lies,
    Its lofty neb looks to the skies:
    The bigger it is the good wife loves 't better,
    She pluckt it and suckt it, till her eyes did water.
    She took it into her hand, and said it was good.
    Put it in her belly and stirred up her blood.

SCALIGER, Julius Caesar (1484–1558)

Italian poet. Latin riddles published in *Poetices* (1561) and *Poemata* (1591).

605. *Ore gero gladium, matrisque in pectore condo*
    Ut mox, qua nunc sunt mortua, viva colas.
    Dux meus a tergo caudamque trahens retrahensque
    Hasta non me ut eam verberat ast alios.

(I carry a sword in my mouth, and I bury it in my mother's breast so that soon you may cultivate, alive, what is now dead. My leader from behind me sticks a tail on me and drags it back and forth, and lashes not me but others, in order to beat her.)

606. *Quale animal, dic, esse putes, quod nobile totum.*
    Est oculus, neque pars praeterea ulla manet?
    Quotidie gignit natum sine matre creatum
    Qui tamen una ipsa hac interit ille die.
    Cuius item soror absente est genitore creata,
    Partita imperium fratris, et interitum.

(Tell me, what creature is this that is excellent in all degrees: is it an eye, with no other part remaining? Every day he is re-born without a mother to give him birth, and every day he dies. And his sister is also reared without a parent, and shares the empire of her brother, and shares his death.)

SCHILLER, Johann Christoph Friedrich von (1759–1805)

German dramatist/poet and leading figure of European Romantic movement. Riddles contained in *Turandot* (1802) and *Parabeln und Rätsel* (1803).

607. It bears thee many a mile away,
    And yet its place it changes ne'er;
    It has no pinions to display,
    And yet conducts thee through the air.

    It is the bark of swiftest motion
    That every weary wanderer bore;

With speed of thought the greatest ocean
  It carries thee in safety o'er;
  One moment wafts thee to the shore.

608. There stands a dwelling, vast and tall,
  On unseen columns fair;
No wanderer treads or leaves its hall,
  And none can linger there.

Its wondrous structure first was plann'd
  With art no mortal knows;
It lights the lamps with its own hand
  'Mongst which it brightly glows.

It has a roof, as crystal bright,
Form'd of one gem of dazzling light;
  Yet mortal eye has ne'er
  Seen Him who placed it there.

609. Within a well two buckets lie,
  One mounts, and one descends;
When one is full, and rises high,
  The other downward wends.

They wander ever to and fro –
Now empty are, now overflow.
If to the mouth thou liftest *this*,
That hangs within the dark abyss.
In the same moment they can ne'er
Refresh thee with their treasures fair.

610. Know'st thou the form on tender ground?
  It gives itself its glow, its light;
And though each moment changing found,
  Is ever whole and ever bright.
In narrow compass 'tis confin'd,
  Within the smallest frame it lies;
Yet all things great that move thy mind,
  That form alone to thee supplies.

And canst thou, too, the crystal name?
  No gem can equal it in worth;
It gleams, yet kindles ne'er to flame,
  It sucks in even all the earth.
Within its bright and wondrous ring
  Is pictur'd forth the glow of heaven,
And yet it mirrors back each thing
  Far fairer than to it 'twas given.

611. For ages an edifice here has been found,
      It is not a dwelling, it is not a fane;
  A horseman for hundreds of days may ride round,
      Yet the end of his journey he ne'er can attain.

  Full many a century o'er it has pass'd,
      The might of the storm and of time it defies;
  'Neath the rainbow of Heaven stands free to the last, –
      In the ocean it dips, and soars up to the skies.
  It was not vain glory that bade its erection,
  It serves as a refuge, a shield, a protection;
  Its like on the earth never yet has been known
  And yet by man's hand it is fashion'd alone.

612. Amongst all serpents there is one,
      Born of no earthly breed;
  In fury wild it stands alone,
      And in its matchless speed.

  With fearful voice and headlong force
      It rushes on its prey,
  And sweeps the rider and his horse
      In one fell swoop away.

  The highest point it loves to gain;
      And neither bar nor lock
  Its fiery onslaught can restrain;
      And arms – invite its shock.

  It tears in twain like tender grass,
      The strongest forest-tree;
  It grinds to dust the harden'd brass,
      Though stout and firm it be.

  And yet this beast, that none can tame,
      Its threat ne'er twice fulfils;
  It dies in its self-kindled flame,
      And dies e'en when it kills.

613. The tree whereon decay
      All those from mortals sprung, –
  Full old, and yet whose spray
      Is ever green and young;
  To catch the light, it rolls
      Each leaf upon one side;
  The other, black as coals,
      The sun has ne'er descried.

It places on new rings
    As often as it blows;
The age, too, of all things
    To mortal gaze it shows.
Upon its bark so green
    A name oft meets the eye,
Yet 'tis no longer seen,
    When it grows old and dry.
This tree – what can it mean?
    I wait for thy reply.

614. What is the thing esteem'd by few?
    The monarch's hand it decks with pride,
Yet it is made to injure too,
    And to the sword is most allied.

No blood it sheds, yet many a wound
    Inflicts, – gives wealth, yet takes from none;
Has vanquish'd e'en the earth's wide round,
    And makes life's current smoothly run.

The greatest kingdoms it has fram'd,
    The oldest cities rear'd from dust,
Yet war's fierce torch has ne'er inflam'd;
    Happy are they who in it trust!

615. I live within a dwelling of stone,
    There buried in slumber I dally;
Yet, arm'd with a weapon of iron alone,
    The foe to encounter I sally.
At first I'm invisible, feeble, and mean,
    And o'er me thy breath has dominion;
I'm easily drown'd in a rain-drop e'en,
    Yet in victory waxes my pinion.
When my sister, all-powerful, gives me her hand,
To the terrible lord of the world I expand.

616. Upon a disk my course I trace,
    There restlessly for ever flit;
Small is the circuit I embrace,
    Two hands suffice to cover it.
Yet ere that field I traverse, I
    Full many a thousand mile must go,
E'en though with tempest-speed I fly,
    Swifter than arrow from a bow.

617. A bird it is, whose rapid motion
  With eagle's flight divides the air;
 A fish it is, and parts the ocean,
  That bore a greater monster ne'er;
 An elephant it is, whose rider
  On his broad back a tower has put:
 'Tis like the reptile base, the spider,
  Whenever it extends its foot;
 And when, with iron tooth projecting,
  It seeks its own life-blood to drain,
 On footing firm, itself erecting,
  It braves the raging hurricane.

618. A bridge of pearls its form uprears
  High o'er a grey and misty sea;
 E'en in a moment it appears,
  And rises upwards giddily.

 Beneath its arch can find a road
  The loftiest vessel's mast most high,
 Itself hath never borne a load,
  And seems, when thou draw'st near, to fly.

 It comes first with the stream, and goes
  Soon as the wat'ry flood is dried.
 Where may be found this bridge, disclose,
  And who its beauteous form supplied!

STIGLIANI, Tommaso (1573–1651)

Italian poet and enigmatographer. Riddles contained in *Rime* (1601),
deemed worthy of placing on the Vatican's *Index librorum prohibitorum* in
1605. A cleaned-up version, *Canzoniero*, appeared
in 1623.

619. *Se ben nessun mi batte, io grido forte,*
 Ed hò barba di carne, e bocca d'osso.
 Sto fra Christiani, e per tenermi posso,
 Com'il gran Turco, più d'una Consorte.
 Son crestoso in un luogo, e di tal sorte,
 Che giù mi pendon, quad'il peso è grosso,
 E sempre, ò che mi fermi, ò che sia mosso,
 Avien, che l'horologio in gola porte.
 Son Capitan d'essercito pedone,
 E per usare una mia foggia sgherra
 L'elmo hò in testa, ed in groppa un pennacchione.
 Son senza braccia, e con altrui fò guerra;
 Son senza denti, e mozzico in tenzone;

Porto gli sproni, e vò co i piè per terra.
    Canto spesso sotterra,
Per trovar mia ventura, e mio destino:
E pur stimo un Rubin men d'un Lupino.

(Even if no one beats me, I cry loudly, and I have a beard of flesh and a mouth of bone. I live amongst Christians but, like the grand Turk, I can keep more than one consort. I have a crest in such a place, and of such a kind, that it hangs down from me when its weight is heavy and always, whether I am still or moving, I carry a clock in my throat. I am the captain of an army of foot-soldiers and, to look like a real desperado, I have a helmet on my head and on my back a great plume. I am without arms, yet I make war on others; I am without teeth, yet I tear others to pieces in combat; I wear spurs, yet I go with my feet on the ground. I often sing underground, to find my fortune and my destiny: and yet I value a ruby less than a lupin.)

620. *Hò cent'occhi e non vedo,*
    Son senza groppa, e siedo,
    Mangio d'un cibo, e mai non hò appetito.
    Con le palpebre il trito,
    E con gli occhi il trangugio poco appresso:
    Vomitandol per dietro a un tempo stesso.

(I have a hundred eyes and yet I cannot see; I have no back and yet I sit down; I eat food and yet I have no appetite. I chew with my eyelids and swallow with my eyes whilst vomiting behind at the same time.)

STRAPAROLA, Giovanni Francesco (d. c. 1557)

Italian novelist. Riddles contained in *Tredeci Piacevoli Notti* (1557).

621. In a prison pent forlorn,
    A tiny son to me was born.
    Ah, cruel fate! The savage elf,
    Scarce bigger than a mite himself,
    Devoured me in his ravenous lust,
    And changed me into sordid dust.
    A mother fond I was of late,
    Now worse e'en than a slave's my fate.

622. In the middle of the night,
    Rises one with beard bedight.
    Though no astrologer he be,
    He marks the hours which pass and flee;
    He wears a crown, although no king;

No priest, yet he the hour doth sing;
Though spurred at heel, he is no knight;
No wife he calls his own by right,
Yet children many round him dwell.
Sharp wits you need this thing to tell.

623. A useful thing, firm, hard, and white,
Outside in shaggy robe bedight;
Hollowed within right cleverly,
It goes to work both white and dry.
When after labour it comes back,
You'll find it moist and very black;
For service it is ready ever,
And fails the hand that guides it never.

624. Of lovers mine is sure the best;
He holds me close upon his breast;
He fondles me; our lips then meet
With kisses and caressing sweet;
His tongue my mouth in fondness seeks,
And with such tender accent speaks,
That hearts with love are all afire.
But brief the space of our desire;
For soon his lips from mine must stray,
To wipe the dews of toil away;
And from me gently he doth move.
Now say, is this the end of love?

625. Left in peace I never move;
But should a foe desire to prove
His mettle on me, straight I fly
Right over wall and roof-tree high.
If driven by a stroke of might,
I take, though wingless, upward flight;
No feet have I, yet 'tis my way
To jump and dance both night and day;
No rest I feel what time my foe
May will that I a-flying go.
No end and no beginning mine,
So strange my nature and design,
And they who see me on the wing
May deem me well a living thing,

626. In a flowering meadow green,
A lovely gentle thing is seen;
Gorgeous be its robes to view,
Bright with yellow, green, and blue.

174

It wears upon its head a crown,
And proudly paces up and down;
Its splendid train it raises high,
And seeks its love with jealous cry;
But gazing at its feet below,
It shrieks aloud for shame and woe.

627. Twofold be we in our name,
But single-natured all the same;
Made with skill and art amain,
And perfected with bitter pain.
Fair dames our service meanly prize,
And poor folk like us large in size.
To countless men we lend our aid,
And never our hard fate upbraid;
But when our useful task is done,
No thanks we get from anyone.

628. In the ground my head is buried,
Yet with care I'm never harried.
In my early youth and fresh,
White and tender is my flesh,
Green my tail; of lowly plight,
The rich man's scorn, the boor's delight.
The peasant on me sets good store,
The noble casts me from his door.

629. From everyone I something take,
But on myself no claim I make.
Mark well my nature. If you gaze
Into my face I mock your ways:
For if you sorrow, I am sad;
But if you smile, you make me glad.
Because I tell truth from a lie,
Men call me wicked, false, and sly;
Strange saying this, but true I ween.
So I, to let it clear be seen
That truth nor honesty I lack,
Will never tell you white is black.

630. A proud and cruel maid I spied,
As through the flowery meads she hied.
Behind her trailed a lengthy train,
Upreared her head in high disdain.
And swiftly on her way she took,
And sharp her touch, and eke her look.
What though her tongue moves all around,

She utters neither voice nor sound.
She is long, and thin, and wise,
He can tell her name who tries.

631. My lady seats her in a chair,
And raises then her skirt with care;
And as I know she waits for me,
I bring her what she fain would see,
Then soft I lift her dainty leg,
Whereon she cries, 'Hold, hold, I beg!
It is too strait, and eke too small;
Be gentle, or you'll ruin all.'
And so to give her smallest pain,
I try once more, and eke again.

632. Gentle dames, I go to find
What aye to me is blithe and kind,
And having found it, next I ween
I set it straight my knees between;
And then I rouse the life that dwells
Within, and soon its virtue tells.
As to and fro my hand I sway,
Beneath my touch sweet ardours play –
Delights which might a savage move,
And make you faint through too much love.

SWIFT, Jonathan (1667–1745)
Irish satirist. Riddles published in various literary magazines.

633. In Youth exalted high in Air,
Or bathing in the Waters fair;
Nature to form me took Delight,
And clad my Body all in White:
My Person tall, and slender Waste,
On either Side with Fringes grac'd;
Till me that Tyrant Man espy'd,
And drag'd me from my Mother's Side:
No Wonder now I look so thin;
The Tyrant strip't me to the Skin:
My Skin he flay'd, my Hair he cropt;
At Head and Foot my Body lopt:
And then, with Heart more hard than Stone,
He pick't my Marrow from the Bone.
To vex me more, he took a Freak,
To slit my Tongue, and made me speak:
But, that which wonderful appears,

I speak to Eyes and not to Ears.
He oft employs me in Disguise,
And makes me tell a Thousand Lyes:
To me he chiefly gives in Trust
To please his Malice, or his Lust.
From me no Secret he can hide;
I see his Vanity and Pride:
And my Delight is to expose
His Follies to his greatest Foes.

All Languages I can command,
Yet not a Word I understand.
Without my Aid, the best Divine
In Learning would not know a Line:
The Lawyer must forget his Pleading,
The Scholar could not shew his Reading.
Nay; Man, my Master, is my Slave:
I give Command to kill or save.
Can grant ten Thousand Pounds a Year,
And make a Beggar's Brat a Peer.

But, while I thus my Life relate,
I only hasten on my Fate.
My Tongue is black, my Mouth is furr'd,
I hardly now can force a Word.
I dye unpity'd and forgot;
And on some Dunghill left to rot.

634. All-ruling Tyrant of the Earth,
To vilest Slaves I owe my Birth.
How is the greatest Monarch blest,
When in my gaudy Liv'ry drest!
No haughty Nymph has Pow'r to run
From me; or my Embraces shun.
Stabb'd to the Heart, condemned to Flame,
My Constancy is still the same.
The fav'rite Messenger of *Jove*,
And *Lemnian* God consulting strove,
To make me glorious to the Sight
Of Mortals, and the Gods Delight.
Soon would their Altars Flame expire,
If I refus'd to lend them Fire.

635. By Fate *exalted high* in Place;
Lo, here I stand with *double Face*;
Superior none on Earth I find;
But see *below me* all Mankind.

Yet, as it oft attends the Great,
I almost *sink* with my own *Weight*;
At every *Motion* undertook,
The Vulgar all consult my *Look*.
I sometimes give Advice in *Writing*,
But never of my own *inditing*.

    I am a Courtier in my Way;
For those who *rais'd* me, I *betray*;
And some give out, that I entice
To Lust and Luxury, and Dice:
Who Punishments on me inflict,
Because they find their Pockets pick't.

    By riding *Post* I lose my Health;
And only to get others Wealth.

636. Though I, alas! a Pris'ner be,
My Trade is, Pris'ners to set free.
No Slave his Lord's Commands obeys,
With such *insinuating* Ways.
My Genius *piercing, sharp* and *bright*,
Wherein the Men of Wit delight.
The Clergy keep me for their Ease,
And *turn* and *wind* me as they please.
A new and wond'rous Art I show
Of raising Spirits from below;
In *Scarlet* some, and some in *White*;
They rise, walk round, yet never fright.
In at each *Mouth* the *Spirits* pass,
Distinctly seen as through a Glass:
O'er *Head* and *Body* make a Rout,
And drive at last all *Secrets* out:
And still, the more I show my Art,
The more they *open every Heart*.

    A greater Chymist none, than I,
Who from *Materials hard and dry*,
Have taught Men to *extract* with Skill,
More precious Juice than from a Still.

    Although I'm often *out of Case*,
I'm not asham'd to show my *Face*,
Though at the Tables of the Great,
I near the Side-board take my Seat;
Yet, the plain Squire, when Dinner's done,
Is never pleas'd till I make one:

He kindly bids me near him stand;
And often takes me by the *Hand*.

 I twice a Day a *hunting* go;
Nor ever fail to *seize my Foe*;
And, when I have him by the *Pole*,
I drag him upwards from his *Hole*.
Though some are of so stubborn Kind,
I'm forc'd to leave a *Limb* behind.

 I hourly wait some fatal End;
For, I can *break*, but scorn to *bend*.

637. Begotten, and Born, and dying with Noise,
The Terror of Women, and Pleasure of Boys,
Like the Fiction of Poets concerning the Wind,
I'm chiefly unruly, when strongest confin'd.
For Silver and Gold I don't trouble my Head,
But all I delight in is Pieces of Lead;
Except when I trade with a Ship or a Town,
Why then I make pieces of Iron go down.
One Property more I would have you remark,
No Lady was ever more fond of a Spark;
The Moment I get one my Soul's all a-fire,
And I roar out my Joy, and in Transport expire.

638. There is a Gate, we know full well,
That stands 'twixt Heav'n, and Earth, and Hell,
Where many for a Passage venture,
But very few are found to enter;
Altho' 'tis open Night and Day,
They for that Reason shun this Way:
Both Dukes and Lords abhor its Wood,
They can't come near it for their Blood.
What other Way they take to go,
Another Time I'll let you know.
Yet Commoners with greatest Ease,
Can find an Entrance when they please.
The poorest hither march in State,
(Or they can never pass the Gate)
Like *Roman* Generals triumphant,
And then they take a Turn and jump on't.
If gravest Parsons here advance,
They cannot pass before they dance;
There's not a Soul, that does resort here,
But strips himself to pay the Porter.

639. I am jet-Black, as you may see,
     The Son of Pitch, and gloomy Night;
     Yet all that know me will agree,
        I'm dead except I live in Light.

     Sometimes in Panegyrick high,
        Like lofty *Pindar* I can soar,
     And raise a Virgin to the Sky,
        Or sink her to a pocky Whore.

     My Blood this Day is very sweet,
        To-morrow of a bitter Juice,
     Like Milk 'tis cry'd about the Street,
        And so apply'd to diff'rent Use.

     Most wond'rous is my Magick Power;
        For with one Colour I can paint;
     I'll make the Dev'l a Saint this Hour,
        Next make a Devil of a Saint.

     Thro' distant Regions I can fly,
        Provide me but with Paper Wings,
     And fairly shew a Reason, why
        There shou'd be Quarrels among Kings.

     And after all you'll think it odd,
        When learned Doctors will dispute,
     That I shou'd point the Word of GOD,
        And shew where they can best confute.

     Let Lawyers bawl and strain their Throats,
        'Tis I that must the Lands convey,
     And strip their Clients to their Coats;
        Nay give their very Souls away.

640. We are little airy Creatures,
     All of diff'rent Voice and Features,
     One of us in Glass is set,
     One of us you'll find in Jet,
     T'other you may see in Tin,
     And the fourth a Box within,
     If the fifth you shou'd pursue
     It can never fly from you.

641. Never speaking, still awake,
     Pleasing most when most I speak,
     The Delight of old and young,
     Tho' I speak without a Tongue.
     Nought but one Thing can confound me,

180

Many Voices joining round me;
Then I fret, and rave and gabble,
Like the Labourers of *Babel*.
Now I am a Dog, or Cow,
I can bark, or I can low,
I can bleat, or I can sing,
Like the Warblers of the Spring.
Let the Love-sick Bard complain,
And I mourn the cruel Pain;
Let the happy Swain rejoice,
And I join my helping Voice;
Both are welcome, Grief or Joy,
I with either sport and toy.
Tho' a Lady, I am stout,
Drums and Trumpets bring me out;
Then I clash and roar, and rattle,
Join in all the Din of Battle.
Jove, with all his loudest Thunder,
When I'm vext, can't keep me under;
Yet so tender is my Ear,
That the lowest Voice I fear;
Much I dread the Courtier's Fate,
When his Merit's out of Date,
For I hate a silent Breath,
And a Whisper is my Death.

642. We are little Brethren twain,
Arbiters of Loss and Gain,
Many to our Counters run,
Some are made, and some undone.
But, Men find it to their Cost,
Few are made, but Numbers lost.
Tho' we play them Tricks for ever,
Yet, they always hope, our Favour.

643. By something form'd, I nothing am,
Yet ev'ry Thing that you can name;
In no Place have I ever been,
Yet ev'ry where I may be seen;
In all Things false, yet always true,
I'm still the same – but ever new.
Lifeless, Life's perfect Form I wear,
Can shew a Nose, Eye, Tongue, or Ear;
Yet neither Smell, See, Taste, or Hear.
All Shapes and Features I can boast,

No Flesh, no Bones, no Blood – no Ghost:
All Colours, without Paint, put on,
And change like the *Cameleon*.
Swiftly I come, and enter there,
Where not a Chink lets in the Air;
Like Thought I'm in a Moment gone,
Nor can I ever be alone;
All Things on Earth I imitate,
Faster than Nature can create;
Sometimes imperial Robes I wear,
Anon in Beggar's Rags appear;
A Giant now, and strait an Elf,
I'm ev'ry one, but ne'er my self;
Ne'er sad I mourn, ne'er glad rejoice,
I move my Lips, but want a Voice;
I ne'er was born, nor e'er can die,
Then prythee tell me what am I.

SYLVAIN, Alexandre (1535–*c*. 1585)

French pseudonym of Belgian poet Alexander van den Bussche. French
riddles published in *Cinquante aenigmes françoises* (1582).

644.   *I'ai engendré seul deuze beaux enfans,*
Les uns chagrins, les autres triomphans,
Desquels chacun en suivant sa nature,
Sans estre aydé d'aucune creature,
Faict d'engendrer tellement son devoir
Que trente fils beaux & clairs nous faict voir:
Oultre ce fils engendrent trente filles

Brunes: mais tant à concevoir habilles,
Que chacune a son frère pour espoux.
Et nous produict ce marriage doux
Filles encor iusques à deux douzaines,
Desquelles puis naissant aultres certaines
Filles, qui sont soixante & quatre à point:
Devinez qui ie suis, ou ne suis point?

(I have given birth to twelve beautiful children all by myself, some
of them gloomy, others triumphant. Each of them in following his
nature, again without the help of any other creature, performs his
duty in breeding to such an extent that thirty handsome and bright
sons are born. In addition to these sons thirty dark daughters are
conceived so skilfully that each one has her brother for a husband.
And this sweet wedding produces still more daughters for us until
there are two dozen, from whom are conceived certain other

daughters, who number exactly sixty-four [*sic*]. Now see whether
or not you can guess who I am.)

645. *Peintre ne suis, toutesfois je figure*
    Facilement le pourtrait de plusieurs,
    Representant bien au vray les couleurs,
    En tous les poincts requis en pourtraiture.

    Parfois un temps ce mien ouvrage dure,
    Parfois bien peu, non pas les rigueurs
    Du temps, qui fait perir herbes, & fleurs:
    Car tant ne suis subject à pourriture.

    Mais ceux, qui sont cause de mon labeur,
    Sont cause après (voyez mon grand malheur)
    Que plus il n'est, ou bien qu'il ne se monstre.

    Aux femmes suis un tresor precieux,
    Qui bien souvent fait despit à leurs yeux,
    Puis veulent bien, qu'après ie les rencontre.

(I am not a painter, but I can easily create the portrait of several,
representing the true colours and all the things required in
portraiture. Sometimes my work lasts some time, sometimes very
little, but not because of the demands of time which kills the grass
and flowers, for I am not touched by decay. But those who are the
subject of my labours are, afterwards, the cause (see my great
misfortune) of the fact that it no longer exists, or that it does not
show itself. To womankind I am a precious treasure, which none
the less often affronts their eyes. Then they wish that I should meet
them afterwards.)

646.   *Ie n'ay ny pieds, ny mains, ny teste, mais un corps,*
    Qui est tousiours armé d'une armure bien forte
    Qui me sert de rampart, de fenestre, & de porte,
    Et par fois est ouverte à ceux qui par dehors
    Guettent: pour me manger, car plus que moy sont forts.
    Mais pour mieux leur monstrer combien celà m'importe
    Ie les retiens captifs, & prins de telle sorte
    Que malgré leur effort souvent demeurent morts.
    Ie ne les mange point, car ce qu'est ma viande
    Est si tres delicat qu'à peine se peut voir,
    En fin ie suis mangé tant ma misere est grande,
    Qui me sçaura nommer fera bien son devoir.

(I have neither feet, nor hands, nor head, but only a body, which
is always protected by very strong armour that serves as rampart,
window and door, and is sometimes opened to those who are

outside lying in wait: to eat me, for they are stronger than me. But in order to show them how much I resent this, I keep them captive and prisoner so that in spite of all their efforts they often die. But I do not eat them, because the kind of food I eat is so dainty that you can hardly see it. In the end, though, I am eaten and my misery is great. He who can name me will have performed his task well.)

SYLVANO, Alexandro (1535–c. 1585)

Spanish pseudonym of Belgian poet Alexander van den Bussche. Spanish riddles published in *Quarenta aenigmes en lengua espannola* (1581).

647.   *Pregunto quien es aquel cavallero,*
    Rey es forçado que siempre vencio,
    Es entre damas soldato guerrero,
    Segundo en su casa jamas consintio
    De musica, y celos, de amor se mantiene
    De cuerpo es gentil tambien generoso
    Vence à la onça, al tigre, y al osso
    Tambien el lion gran miedo lo tiene.

(I ask you who is that noble gentleman who is compelled to be king but is always vanquished? Amongst ladies he is a warlike soldier and his authority is second to none in his own home. He lives on music, jealousy and love and his body is both graceful and noble in form. He conquers the [onça?], the tiger and the bear and even the lion is afraid of him.)

SYMPHOSIUS (5th century)

Latin poet and father of Anglo-Latin riddling. Once believed to be the minor Roman poet Lactantius or Firmianus Symphosius Caelius. Riddles contained in *Symphosii Aenigmata*.

648. Blind is my face in dark shadows hid; the very day is night nor is any sun by me perceived; I prefer to be covered by clods; thus no one will see me either.

649. None can split me, though many cut me; but I am of changeable hue, at some time hence I shall be white. I prefer to stay black, the less I shall fear my fate.

650. I bring great power from little strength. I open houses when closed up; but again I shut them up when open. I keep the house safe for its owner; yet again I am kept safe by him.

651. I, the god's dear mistress, that dwell near the deep banks, sweetly singing to the Muses, overspread with black hue, I am the herald of my master's tongue when pressed light between his fingers.

652. In winter I depart; when the warmth returns I come back. My offspring I abandon, but another mother rears it. What else do you want me to tell you? My voice betrays me.

653. I was far larger once while life remained; but now I am lifeless after being rent, tied up and plucked away; I am devoted to the soil, yet I am not buried in a tomb.

654. My twin points are joined together by crooked iron; with the wind I wrestle, with the depths of the sea I fight; I search out the midmost water, and I bite the very ground itself.

655. I do not die forthwith when my breath leaves me; for it constantly returns, though as often it departs; and one moment I have a great store of air, the next I have no power at all.

656. A letter was my food, yet I know not what a letter is. In books I have lived, yet I am no more studious on that account. I devoured the Muses, yet so far I have made no progress.

657. I bite those that bite me; of my own accord I bite no one; but though I bite, many are ready to bite me. No one fears my bite, because I have no teeth.

658. Its home is the earth, and it re-echoes with loud voice: the home itself resounds, but the host is mute and makes no sound; both however run, the host and the home run together.

TALMUD, The
Jewish religious text. Riddles occur *passim*.

659. Bake him with his brother, place him in his father, eat him in his son, and then drink his father.

660. What animal has one voice living and seven voices dead?

TATWINE (d. 734)
Archbishop of Canterbury. Riddles contained in *Aenigmata* with those of Eusebius (q.v.).

661. *Efferus exuviis populator me spoliavit,*
   Vitalis pariter flatus spiramina dempsit,
   In planum me iterum campum sed verterat auctor.
   Frugiferos cultor sulcos mox irrigat undis,
   Omnigenam nardi messem mea prata rependunt,
   Qua sanis victum et læsis præstabo medelam.

A ruthless pillager stripped me from a skin and likewise took away the holes through which passed the breath of life; the preparer next pounds me into a level surface; soon the dresser waters the fruitful furrows, my level fields pay back a manifold and fragrant harvest whereby I shall give livelihood to the healthy and healing to the sick.

662. *Celsicolae nascor fœcunda matris in alvo,*
Quæ superas penitus sedes habitare solescit.
Sum petulans agilisque fera, insons corporis astu,
Ardua ceu pennis convecta cacumina scando,
Veloci vitans passu discrimina Martis.

(I was born in the fecund womb of my lofty-dwelling mother who is accustomed to dwelling in the highest haunts. I am a pert and agile creature, harmless and adroit of body. I climb high tree-tops as if carried on wings, avoiding with a swift step the hazards of war.)

663. *Egregius vere nullus sine me est, neque felix;*
Amplector cunctos quorum me corda requirunt.
Qui absque meo graditur comitatu morte peribit;
Et qui me gestat sospes sine fine manebit.
Inferior terris et altior sed cœlis exsto.

(Truly no one is outstanding without me, nor fortunate; I embrace all those whose hearts ask for me. He who goes without me goes about in the company of death; and he who bears me will remain lucky for ever. But I stand lower than earth and higher than heaven.)

THEODECTES of Phaselis (*c.* 375–334 BC)

Ancient Greek orator and poet. Riddles cited in Athenaeus's *Deipnosophistae*.

664. What thing is that which is not among all the things that Earth, the nurse, brings forth, nor the sea, nor has any growth in its limbs like that of things mortal, yet in the time of its earliest begotten generation is largest, but at its midmost height is small, and at old age itself is again largest in shape and size?

665. There be two sisters, of whom the one gives birth to the other, while she herself, after giving birth, is brought forth by the other.

TOLKIEN, J. R. R. (1892–1973)

Professor of English Literature and writer. Riddles occur in *The Hobbit* (1937).

666. What has roots as nobody sees,
   Is taller than the trees,
      Up, up it goes,
      And yet never grows?

667. Voiceless it cries,
   Wingless flutters,
   Toothless bites,
   Mouthless mutters.

668. An eye in a blue face
   Saw an eye in a green face.
   'That eye is like to this eye,'
   Said the first eye,
   'But in low place,
   Not in high place.'

669. It cannot be seen, cannot be felt,
   Cannot be heard, cannot be smelt.
   It lies behind stars and under hills,
      And empty holes it fills.
   It comes first and follows after.
      Ends life, kills laughter.

670. A box without hinges, key, or lid.
   Yet golden treasure inside is hid.

671. Alive without breath,
   As cold as death;
   Never thirsty, ever drinking,
   All in mail never clinking.

672. This thing all things devours:
   Birds, beasts, trees, flowers;
   Gnaws iron, bites steel;
   Grinds hard stones to meal;
   Slays king, ruins town,
   And beats high mountain down.

TRUE TRIAL OF UNDERSTANDING OR WIT NEWLY REVIV'D, THE (18th century)

English chapbook.

673. While I did live, I food did give,
   Which many one did daily eat.
   Now being dead, you see they tread
   Me under feet about the street.

674. Tho' it be cold I wear no cloaths,
   The frost and snow I never fear,
   I value neither shoes nor hose,
   And yet I wander far and near;
   Both meat and drink are always free,
   I drink no cyder, mum, nor beer,

What Providence doth send to me
I neither buy, nor sell, nor lack.

675. Promotion lately was bestow'd
Upon a person mean and small;
Then many persons to him flow'd,
Yet he return'd no thanks at all;
But yet their hands were ready still
To help him with their kind good will.

676. My weapon is exceeding keen,
Of which I think I well may boast,
And I'll encounter Colonel Green
Together with his mighty host.
With me they could not then compare,
I conquer them both great and small,
Tho' thousands stood before me there
I stood and got no harm at all.

677. I saw five birds all in a cage,
Each bird had but one single wing,
They were an hundred years of age,
And yet did fly and sweetly sing.
The wonder did my mind possess,
When I beheld their age and strength;
Besides, as near as I can guess, –
Their tails were thirty feet in length.

678. Stouthearted men with naked knives
Beset my house with all their crew;
If I had ne'er so many lives,
I must be slain and eaten, too.

679. Divided from my brother now,
I am companion for mankind;
I that lately stood for show,
Do now express my master's mind.

UNIVERSAL MAGAZINE OF KNOWLEDGE AND PLEASURE, THE (1747–1815)

English pot-pourri journal appearing monthly. It can be seen with some justification as being perhaps the best representative of English enigmatography in the eighteenth century. Riddles ceased to be published in its pages with the new series commencing in 1814.

680. Of fancy born, by folly bred,
From foreign countries hither led:
My form and shape I often change,

Am really nothing; yet, 'tis strange,
By all caress'd, by all admir'd,
In wealth and poverty desir'd;
Of such variety I'm made,
That I'm the great support of trade;
And tho' brought up by wisdom's foe,
I much of wisdom in me show:
For, by my fleeting changing state,
I make all money circulate;
Reward the sailor for his pains,
And much augment the merchant's gains.
I am no sooner known to be,
Than all the great take leave of me,
And I'm a mere non-entity.
To have me, all, their cares employ,
But when possess'd I quickly cloy:
I serve the ladies when alone,
To shew their handy skill upon,
And when assembled, give them pleasure,
Since I'm their chiefest talking treasure.

681. Before I was by man a prisoner made,
I in green meads and verdant pastures stray'd;
But soon as e'er he me bereft of life,
As soon I caus'd content, as often strife.
Now dead I have no tongue, yet I can speak
All languages, *French, Hebrew, Latin, Greek*:
To most remotest parts my words are sent,
No hands I have, but what to me are lent;
I'm short of stature, my body it is slender;
And oft companion to the fair and tender:
Ladies delight to use me at their leisure,
To tell my name, you'll give the writer pleasure.

682. Behold the *Lilliputian* throng,
Nor male, nor female, old or young;
Four inches tall, of slender size,
With neither mouth, nor nose, nor eyes,
Who never from each other stray,
But stand in order night and day,
Like soldiers marshall'd in array.
A bloody ensign each does bear,
Yet ne'er trained up to feats of war;
Their actions gentler passions move,
And aid and fan the flames of love,

189

Soften the unrelenting fair,
And sooth the pensive statesman's care;
Nimble as thought they skip and dance,
Yet ne'er retreat, nor ne'er advance,
Nor order change – like the world's frame,
Always unalterably the same.
Tho' nimble and to action free,
Yet move they never willingly,
But in their secret caverns sleep,
Time without end, nor stir, nor peep.
Until some heav'n-born genius comes,
To raise them from their sleepy tombs,
By pow'r unseen, then up they spring
Without the help of leg or wing,
And mount; and as they mount they sing.

683. At two days old good *Latin* I speak,
　　Tho' for it I never went to school:
　Arms I have four, which come out of my *back*,
　　And in *yellow* am dress'd like a fool.
All men me seek, tho' few can me get,
　　When caught I'm confin'd like a fish in a net.

684. Here is a thing that *nothing* is
'Tis foolish, wanton, sober, wise;
It hath no wings, no eyes, no ears,
And yet it flies, it sees, it hears:
It lives by loss, it feeds in smart,
It dwells in woe, it liveth not.
Yet ever more this hungry elf,
Doth feed on nothing but itself.

685. When virtue smil'd and spread her purple wings,
O'er senates, laws, and held the crowns of Kings:
How happy I! who, by a just applause,
Converted all to one essential cause, ·
Bid merit rise, and held imperial sway,
Till *Athens* fell: O black and awful day!
Then lofty *Rome* to every virtue prone,
To arts and arms, with heighten'd lustre shone,
Smil'd in the records of immortal fame,
And rais'd a temple sacred to my name;
Approv'd my worth, ador'd my tender care,
And made me guardian to the charming fair.

686. Without edge it cuts; without tongue it sings;
Foams without anger; and flies without wings.

687. Nor wings, nor feet, unto my share have fell,
　　Yet I in swiftness do the best excel.
　　Arms I have none, nor weapons do I wear,
　　And yet I daily wound the brave and fair.
　　My name is odious, both to friends and foes,
　　Yet I'm admired by all the Belles and Beaus.
　　And when my name's concealed, I've many friends,
　　The best man fears me, and his fault amends.
　　All wise men hate me, as their common foe,
　　Take C from me, I keep you from the snow.
　　Old maids caress me, for this world I hate
　　As it hates them, so we receive our fate.
　　From these short hints, to tell my name's your task,
　　That well performed, I've nothing more to ask.

VIRGIL (70–19 BC)

Accepted sobriquet of Publius Vergilius Maro, Roman poet. Riddles occur in the third eclogue of *Pastoral Poems* ('Are these Meliboeus' sheep?').

688. *Damoetas:* Read me this riddle – and I shall take you for Apollo's self. Where in the world is the sky no more than three yards wide?

689. *Menalcas:* Answer me this and Phyllis shall be yours alone. Where in the world do flowers grow with kings' names written on them?

WHATELY, Richard (1787–1863)

Archbishop of Dublin and formerly Professor of Political Economy at Oxford University. Wrote occasional riddles.

690. My *first* is equality, my *second* inferiority; my *whole* superiority.

WHETSTONE FOR DULL WITS, A (18th century)

English chapbook.

691. Into this world I came hanging,
　　　And when from the same I was ganging,
　　I was cruelly batter'd and Squeez'd,
　　　And men with my blood, they were pleas'd.

692. Tho' of great age
　　I'm kept in a Cage
　　Having a long tail and one ear,
　　My mouth it is round
　　And when Joys do abound
　　O' then I sing wonderful clear.

693. The greatest travellers that e'er were known
　　　By Sea and land were mighty archers twain;

No armour proof, or fenced walls of stone,
　　Could turn their arrows; bulwarks were in vain.
Thro' princes courts, and kingdoms far and near,
　　As well in foreign parts as Christendom,
These travellers their weary steps then steer,
　　But to the deserts seldom come.

694. A thing with a thundering breech
　　It weighing a thousand welly,
　　　　I have heard it roar
　　　　Louder than Guys wild boar,
　　They say it hath death in its belly.

695. It flies without wings,
　　Between silken strings
　　And leaves as you'll find
　　Its guts still behind.

696. Close in a cage a bird I'll keep,
　　That sings both day and night,
　　When other birds are fast asleep
　　Its notes yield sweet delight.

697. A Visage fair
　　And voice is rare,
　　Affording pleasant charms;
　　Which is with us
　　Most ominous
　　Presaging future harms.

698. To ease men of their care
　　I do both rend and tear
　　Their mother's bowels still;
　　Yet tho' I do,
　　There are but few
　　That seem to take it ill.

699. By sparks in fine lawn
　　I am lustily drawn,
　　But not in a chariot or Coach;
　　I fly, in a word,
　　More swift than a bird,
　　That does the green forest approach.

700. My back is broad, my belly is thin,
　　And I am sent to pleasure youth;
　　Where mortal man has never been
　　Tho' strange it is a naked truth.

WHEWELL, William (1794–1866)

English philosopher. Wrote occasional riddles.

701. A handless man had a letter to write,
     And he who read it had lost his sight;
     The dumb repeated it word for word,
     And deaf was the man who listened and heard.

WILBERFORCE, Samuel (1805–73)

Bishop of Winchester and son of William Wilberforce. The solution
to this excellent riddle was finally published by Lewis Carroll in 1866.

702. I have a large Box, with two lids, two caps, three established
     Measures, and a great number of articles a Carpenter cannot do
     without. – Then I have always by me a couple of good Fish, and a
     number of a smaller tribe, – besides two lofty Trees, fine Flowers,
     and the fruit of an indigenous Plant; a handsome Stag; two playful
     Animals; and a number of a smaller and less tame Herd: – Also two
     Halls, or Places of Worship; some Weapons of warfare; and many
     Weathercocks: – The Steps of an Hotel; The House of Commons
     on the eve of a Dissolution; Two Students or Scholars, and some
     Spanish Grandees, to wait upon me.
         All pronounce me a wonderful piece of Mechanism, but few
     have numbered up the strange medley of things which compose
     my whole.

WYATT, Sir Thomas (1503–42)

English poet and diplomat. Wrote occasional riddles, published
in *Tottel's Miscellany* (1557).

703. Vulcan begat me; Minerva me taught:
     Nature, my mother; Craft nourisht me year by year:
     Three bodies are my foode: my strength is nought.
     Anger, wrath, waste, and noise are my children dear.
     Guess, my friend, what I am: and how I am wraught:
     Monster of sea, or of land, or of elsewhere.
     Know me, and use me: and I may thee defend:
     And if I be thine enemy, I may thy life end.

704. One is my sire: my soons, twise six they bee:
     Of daughters each of them begets, you see,
     Twise ten: whereof one sort be fayr of face,
     The oother doth unseemly black disgrace.
     Nor this hall rout is thrall unto deathdaye,
     Nor worn with wastfull time, but live alwaye:
     And the same alwaies (straunge case) do dye.

The fire, the daughters, and the soons distry.
In case you can so hard a knot unknit:
You shall I count an Edipus in wit.

YORKSHIRE HOUSEHOLD RIDDLES

A series of folk riddles submitted by readers and published in *Notes and Queries* (October 1865).

705. Goes up white and comes down yellow.

706. As I were going over London Brig,
   I met a load of hay,
I shot wi' my pistol,
   And all flew away.

707. Black and breet [bright],
   Runs without feet.

708. All round t' house,
   All round t' house
And it [in the] cupboard.

709. As I were going over London Brig,
   I pipp't into a winder,
And I saw four-and-twenty ladies,
   Dancing on a cinder.

Solutions to the Riddles

1. man on a horse
2. lice, fingers, eyes
3. dog
4. flying fish
5. salt
6. whetstone
7. Minotaur
8. stork
9. cuirass
10. gadfly
11. water spider
12. ostrich
13. leech
14. fire
15. milfoil (yarrow)
16. heliotrope
17. candle
18. beaver
19. pen
20. dagger
21. bubble
22. dove
23. cat
24. fish
25. glass cup
26. pregnant sow
27. man blind from birth
28. serpent
29. woman in labour with twins
30. spark
31. sleep
32. bread and flint
33. *punkah* (a canvas ventilating fan)
34. rope of palm fibre
35. reed pen
36. water-wheel
37. fingernail
38. wine
39. *uqâb* ('a black eagle' and also 'a standard')
40. *saur* ('a bullock' and also 'a piece of cheese')
41. barrel of beer
42. tadpole
43. needle and pin
44. clock
45. bottle
46. potato
47. shoe
48. saw
49. glove
50. stockings
51. wig
52. cabbage
53. track
54. bed
55. frog
56. squirrel
57. moon
58. moon
59. potatoes
60. tomorrow
61. riddle
62. pencil
63. river
64. road
65. milk

66. breath
67. smoke
68. bucket in a well
69. voice
70. sun
71. woman crossing a bridge with a pail on her head
72. man with sods on his head
73. egg in duck's belly
74. wind
75. nail in horseshoe
76. an axe on a man's shoulder
77. bark of a tree
78. path
79. sun
80. rain
81. bird in a cage
82. sawmill
83. fire
84. turnstile
85. match
86. ear of corn
87. river
88. river
89. shoe
90. saw
91. chair
92. shoe
93. Mississippi
94. 500 pairs of trousers
95. dust
96. snow melted by the sun
97. gun
98. hare
99. bellows
100. clothes horse
101. thimble, finger, needle
102. spectacles
103. milk
104. shoe
105. shoe
106. man sitting on a three-legged stool milking cow is kicked by cow, so man hits cow with stool
107. stars
108. parchment, quill pen, wax
109. bellows
110. shuttle
111. broom
112. grasshopper
113. wheelbarrow
114. cock
115. pocket watch
116. snail
117. duck in a puddle
118. fart
119. 'first it is *cradled*, then it is *threshed* and then it becomes the *flour* of the family'
120. quill pen
121. cask
122. key
123. fire in the grate
124. water
125. book
126. towel
127. gun
128. horseshoe-maker
129. orange
130. pump
131. mirror
132. dead ashes falling on the fire
133. fire and kettle
134. bees
135. watermelon
136. fire: spark, smoke, ashes
137. bees making honey
138. flax
139. carriage wheels
140. man in coffin is dry, bearers are wet
141. ship at anchor (the leaves are its sails)
142. the twelve months of the year

143. icicle
144. paper and ink
145. washed in dew, dried in sunshine
146. sawdust
147. egg
148. wedding ring
149. sieve
150. cabbage
151. candles (unlit and lit)
152. newspaper
153. your name
154. your word
155. milkman's horse
156. umbrella
157. breath
158. silence
159. wedding ring
160. a hole
161. a debt
162. school
163. the letter M
164. footsteps
165. peace
166. an iron pot
167. hair
168. an equal
169. reflection in a mirror
170. nail in the bottom of a ship
171. pump
172. bee
173. grasshopper
174. riddle
175. Red Sea, Moses' rod, the destruction of Pharaoh's host
176. plough
177. water
178. child in her womb
179. embroidery table
180. air
181. snake
182. windmill
183. flea
184. fire
185. spoon
186. egg
187. sight
188. pipe
189. snake
190. tree stump with snow on it
191. hair
192. lobster
193. death
194. apple
195. sponge
196. red-hot poker
197. lobster
198. carpet
199. sheep
200. fiddle
201. hedgehog
202. bell
203. fish caught in a net
204. cock
205. wind
206. bed
207. magpie
208. tongs
209. nettle
210. river
211. egg
212. coffin
213. my son
214. a mountain (it has mountaineers!)
215. charcoal
216. kitten
217. watch
218. cat
219. counterfeit money
220. map
221. chestnut
222. housefly
223. letter with a seal
224. runner beans
225. flax

226. egg
227. clock
228. bridge
229. cradle
230. candle-snuffers
231. fire, smoke
232. water, fire, earth, wind
233. cherry
234. cobweb
235. snail
236. bird
237. health
238. mother's milk
239. swallow's nest
240. woman on a horse beneath a cherry tree with a child at her breast – she eats, the child eats, a bird in the tree eats and the horse grazes
241. Eve
242. rain
243. spider
244. coffee
245. tobacco
246. horseshoe
247. shears
248. bean
249. vine
250. Jonah in the whale
251. bed
252. because it draws and colours beautifully
253. echo
254. because all the rest are inaudible (in audible)
255. chestnut
256. sponge
257. swallow
258. soul
259. goad
260. snail
261. sandal
262. dove, olive leaf, Noah's ark
263. Jonah in the whale's belly
264. hair rope
265. Eve
266. Abindon (or Abingdon), Berkshire
267. Eve
268. heroine
269. pen
270. a letter (the 'babes' are the words)
271. river and fish
272. papyrus
273. ships
274. anchor
275. sponge
276. mirror
277. serpent (land, sea, constellation)
278. courtship
279. wisdom
280. wind
281. ice
282. horse drawn by a pen
283. wheat
284. ship
285. olive
286. pitch
287. (solutions given in text)
288. flea
289. thorn in a man's foot
290. turning a spit
291. eglantine berry
292. playing cards
293. three flies trapped in a glass covered with a slice of bread
294. the ass that bore Mary out of Egypt
295. bee
296. hole in shoe
297. walnut
298. rope-maker
299. pillow-case
300. a rope

301. worm
302. two millstones
303. church, steeple, bell, clapper
304. flame of a candle
305. Eve and her children
306. Noah's ark
307. snail
308. dice
309. walnut
310. sails of a windmill
311. game of bowls
312. feather
313. swan
314. man with spectacles
315. comb and louse killed on its back
316. a hand with rings (except on middle finger)
317. at the bottom of a well
318. icicle
319. spider's web
320. workmen carrying ladders
321. moon
322. hail
323. the speaker
324. bee
325. a woman's girdle
326. peacock's tail
327. parrot in a cage
328. flea
329. horse
330. oyster
331. Galatea (gala-tea)
332. season (sea-son)
333. tablet
334. wine
335. jealousy
336. riddle
337. man with fetters on his legs
338. candle-snuffer
339. Eve
340. snow
341. apple

342. nut
343. arrow
344. knife going into a sheath
345. seed
346. eye
347. John baptizing Jesus
348. days, months, Christian feasts, year
349. 'the horse when it farted in Noah's ark'
350. darkness
351. stone
352. egg
353. peppercorn
354. bees in a hive, honey
355. rose
356. tongue
357. crop in a field
358. cat and bacon
359. year, months, days and nights
360. kiss
361. flute
362. drum
363. the earth
364. coffin
365. dew
366. 'Because when they see the altars covered they think their masters go thither to dinner'
367. 'Because he knoweth not his bed's head from the feet'
368. sack
369. hot water
370. a bridge
371. 'Because their mother is no more maiden'
372. 'When the gander is on her back'
373. 'Cain when he slew his brother Abel'
374. bowl

375. *j'ay assez obey à elle*
376. *cinqs coqs chastrez sont cinq chapons*
377. *trop subtils sont souvent bien surpris*
378. *le souhait en suspens le coeur soustient*
379. *j'ay grand appetit de soupper pour substenter mes appetits*
380. *deux coeurs en un coeur et s'entre-aymer iusques à la fin comme au commencement*
381. *il faut dix né comme souspé*
382. *amendez-vous, qu'attendez-vous la mort*
383. *bonne entreprise fait bon entreprendre*
384. Adam
385. 'A man's sins and his Lord's anger'
386. judgement
387. earth, fire, hell, avaricious man
388. the rump
389. thistle-down
390. quill pen
391. cross
392. cuckoo
393. leather
394. plough
395. onion
396. mead
397. gnats
398. shield
399. key
400. dough
401. bookmoth
402. anchor
403. swan
404. horn
405. rake
406. Hebrew פרדה (= she-mule) remove ד (pronounced דלת =

door), and there remains פרה (= heifer)
407. Hebrew שלשים (= 30) take the ל (= 30), and the remainder is ששם (= 60)
408. taper/candle
409. the letter H
410. year
411. day and night
412. the world (cypresses = 'two halves of heaven'; bird = the sun; nest = zodiacal sign of the ram; death)
413. watch
414. herring (her-ring)
415. riddle
416. ship
417. a man's mind
418. 'Men travelling in the snow are beaten with it, and carry the dead bodies on their garments untill they come to a fire, which makes them vanish away'
419. lute
420. pair of shears
421. mulberry
422. smoke ('pupils' = pupils in eyes)
423. double flute (sailors = fingers)
424. Rhodes (*dos* = 'give')
425. louse
426. clyster
427. Nessus the centaur, with whose blood the robe that slew Heracles was poisoned
428. Eteocles and Polynices, the sons of Oedipus
429. day and night
430. sandal/scandal
431. clyster
432. mirror

433. writing tablet ('Ares' = stylus)
434. pitch
435. mirror
436. sleep ('untruthful' because, though unreal, dreams portend realities)
437. raisin
438. hourglass
439. cat
440. pair of shoes
441. squirrel
442. drum
443. grain of wheat
444. pen
445. sky
446. needle
447. ale
448. dew
449. goldsmith's hammer
450. fog
451. anchor
452. 'A raven always lives in high mountains, and dew falls in deep valleys, a fish lives without breathing, and the booming waterfall is never silent'
453. leek
454. hail and rain
455. sow with nine piglets
456. arrow
457. spider
458. a game of chess
459. ptarmigan
460. cow
461. spark
462. embers in the hearth
463. Jacob and Esau in their mother's womb
464. the pillar of salt Lot's wife became
465. smoke
466. egg, silkworm, cocoon, butterfly
467. bell (which is cast in the earth)
468. eye
469. 'snot of ther noses'
470. dishcloth
471. leaves of a tree
472. 'a yong man in a tavern drinking a Gill of sack to chear up his spirits & so obtained his will'
473. gooseberry
474. 'a rose bud whose outward green leaves are some jaged others plaine'
475. lice
476. stove
477. year
478. Ilo is the speaker's dog out of whose skin he has made shoes and gloves
479. hand
480. watermelon
481. pen
482. candle
483. shadow
484. orange
485. Andrew
486. water under the boat
487. egg
488. snow
489. rain
490. sweeping brush (made of horsehair)
491. the letter R
492. coffin
493. leather
494. cod
495. (solutions given in text)
496. death
497. mirror
498. cock

499. flute
500. mushroom
501. fashion
502. grain of mustard
503. *étoile* (star), *toile* (tablecloth)
504. *ouie* (ear), *oui* (yes)
505. pipe
506. *potage* (soup), *otage* (hostage) *Tage* (river Tagus), *âge* (age)
507. *café* (coffee)
508. *lin* (flax), *Nil* (river Nile)
509. rainbow
510. shadow
511. coal
512. fog/mist
513. holly
514. robin
515. pair of shoes
516. parrot
517. candle
518. tree
519. star
520. needle and thread
521. hedgehog
522. teeth and gums
523. ice
524. plum pudding
525. squirrel
526. the letter A
527. cherry
528. shuttlecock
529. the sun
530. boy's kite
531. eunuch, bat, fennel, pumice
532. (solutions given in text)
533. fire poker
534. bridge
535. bull
536. bell
537. childhood
538. mouse
539. the letter S
540. bellows

541. Frances Sargent Osgood
542. Sarah Anna Lewis (Poe's patroness)
543. (line 1) Spenser; (2) Homer; (3–4) Aristotle; (5–6) Kallimachos; (7–8) Shelley; (9) Pope; (10) Euripides; (11) Mark Akenside; (12) Samuel Roger; (13–14) Euripides; – which together spell 'Shakspeare' [*sic*]
544. scales
545. hope
546. blood
547. Turandot
548. because they are constantly *crossing the line* and running from *pole* to *pole*
549. because it doesn't '*No*' anything
550. because it runs on sleepers
551. because he's eaten out of house and home
552. because it's a *caw's way*
553. because it has a lot of larks
554. because it grows down
555. because the sooner it's *put out* the better
556. because it's light when it rises
557. because it never eats less than a peck
558. when it is rung for dinner
559. because one becomes a woman, the other doesn't
560. when she takes a *fly* that brings her to the Bank
561. ice and water
562. fur glove
563. lark
564. tree
565. sun
566. key
567. tea-kettle

568. bees
569. watch
570. 'Seven are the days of a woman's defilement;
Nine are the months of pregnancy;
Two are the breasts that yield the draught;
And one the child that drinks.'
571. 'That enclosure is the womb; the ten doors are the ten orifices of man – his eyes, ears, nostrils, mouth, the apertures for the discharge of the excreta and the urine, and the navel; when the child is in the embryonic state, the navel is open and the other orifices are closed, but when it issues from the womb, the navel is closed and the others are opened.'
572. Lot's daughter speaking to her son
573. black weevil in a white bean
574. riddle
575. riddle
576. siren
577. day and night
578. smoke
579–582. (solutions given in text)
583. man
584. noise
585. pack of cards
586. yard rule
587. wind/vacuum
588. sea
589. coin
590. letters of the alphabet
591. feather fan
592. two horses, coachman, four wheels, coach, four passengers

593. butterfly
594. bell
595. gnat
596. needle
597. candle
598. candle
599. lightning/wind
600. body and soul/Agni
601. sun
602. year, months, days and nights
603. portrait
604. onion
605. plough
606. day and night
607. telescope
608. cosmos/universe
609. day and night
610. eye
611. Great Wall of China
612. lightning
613. the year
614. plough
615. spark
616. shadows on a sundial
617. ship
618. rainbow
619. cock
620. grater
621. bean and worm
622. cock
623. pen
624. trumpet
625. tennis ball
626. peacock
627. scissors
628. leek
629. mirror
630. serpent
631. tight shoe
632. viol da gamba
633. pen
634. gold

635. gold
636. corkscrew
637. cannon
638. gallows
639. ink
640. the vowels
641. echo
642. pair of dice
643. reflection in a mirror
644. year
645. mirror
646. oyster
647. cock
648. mole
649. hair
650. key
651. reed (from which a flute can be made)
652. cuckoo
653. soldier's boot
654. anchor
655. bellows
656. bookworm
657. onion
658. river and fish
659. i.e., bake the fish in salt, its brother (for salt water comes with the fish from the sea), place him in his father (in water), eat him in his son (i.e. the juice or gravy), and then take a draught of water
660. ibis
661. parchment
662. squirrel
663. humility
664. shadow
665. night and day
666. mountain
667. wind
668. sun and daisy
669. dark
670. egg

671. fish
672. time
673. cow
674. herring in the sea
675. man in pillory
676. man scything grass
677. bells in a steeple
678. oyster
679. ox horn
680. fashion
681. quill pen
682. harpsichord
683. guinea
684. the mind
685. wisdom
686. 'bottle-ale'
687. scandal
688. at the bottom of a well or on a celestial globe
689. hyacinthus (the plant which grew from the spot where the youth Hyacinthus accidentally died; the event recurred at the death of Ajax – the letters in question are AI AI which form part of the plant's colouring and are Greek for an expression of grief)
690. peerless (peer-less)
691. cider apple
692. bell (tail = rope, ear = wheel)
693. Death and Cupid
694. cannon
695. weaver's shuttle
696. clock
697. mermaid
698. plough
699. arrow
700. kite
701. (answer lacking)
702. 'The WHOLE, – is MAN.

The PARTS are as follows:

A large box – The Chest.

Two lids – The Eye lids.

Two Caps – The Knee caps.

Three established Measures – The nails, hands, and feet.

A great number of articles a Carpenter cannot do without – Nails.

A couple of good Fish – The Soles of the Feet.

A number of a smaller tribe – The Muscles (Mussels).

Two lofty Trees – The Palms (of the hands).

Fine Flowers – Two lips (Tulips), and Irises.

The fruit of an indigenous Plant – Hips.

A handsome Stag – The Heart (Hart).

Two playful Animals – The Calves.

A number of a smaller and less tame Herd – The Hairs (Hares).

Two Halls, or Places of Worship – The Temples.

Some Weapons of Warfare – The Arms, and Shoulder blades.

Many Weathercocks – The Veins (Vanes).

The Steps of an Hotel – The Insteps (Inn-Steps).

The House of Commons on the eve of a Dissolution – Eyes and Nose (Ayes and Noes).

Two Students or Scholars – The Pupils of the Eye.

Some Spanish Grandees – The Tendons (Ten Dons).'

703. gun
704. year
705. egg
706. bird
707. an iron
708. mouse
709. sparks

Further Reading

A comprehensive bibliography would be out of place in a book of this nature, even if space would permit it. However, listed below are a few of the more accessible reference works on the history of riddles and riddling, which are given here both to acknowledge a debt in the preparation of the present volume and perhaps also to stimulate the interested reader to further study.

Aristotle, *Poetics*, 22 (many editions available)

De Filippis, Michele, *The Literary Riddle in Sixteenth-century Italy*, University of California Publications in Modern Philology, 1948

—— *The Literary Riddle in Seventeenth-century Italy*, University of California Publications in Modern Philology, 1953

—— *The Literary Riddle in Eighteenth-century Italy*, University of California Publications in Modern Philology, 1967

Opie, Iona and Opie, Peter, *The Lore and Language of Schoolchildren*, Oxford University Press, 1959

Taylor, Archer, *Bibliography of Riddles*, Helsinki, 1939 (this is very comprehensive and covers both books and journals from all over the world from the earliest times to 1939)

—— *English Riddles from Oral Tradition*, University of California Press, 1951

—— *The Literary Riddle before 1600*, University of California Press, 1948

Tupper, Frederick, *The Riddles of the Exeter Book*, Ginn & Co., 1910 (this contains a thorough study of riddling up to 1910 together with the text and detailed analysis of the *Exeter Book* enigmas)

Acknowledgements

Grateful acknowledgement is made for the use of the copyright material as follows: to George Allen & Unwin (Publishers) for *The Hobbit* by J. R. R. Tolkien; Cambridge University Press for *Stories and Ballads of the Far Past*, translated by N. Kershaw; Faber & Faber for *A Choice of Anglo-Saxon Verse*, edited and translated by R. Hamer, and *The Elder Edda*, translated by P. B. Taylor and W. H. Auden; The Folio Society for *The Exeter Book*, translated by K. Crossley-Holland; Gordon Fraser for *The Demaundes Joyous*; Ginn & Co. for *Select Translations of Old English Poetry*, by A. S. Cook and C. B. Tinker; The Loeb Classical Library (Harvard University Press: William Heinemann) for Plutarch's *Dinner of the Seven Wise Men*, Aulus Gellius's *Noctes Atticae*, Petronius's *Satyricon*, Athenaeus's *Deipnosophistae*, Aristophanes's *Wasps*, *The Greek Anthology*; Oxford University Press for *Earliest English Poetry*, by C. W. Kennedy; Penguin Books for Rabelais's *Gargantua & Pantagruel*, translated by J. M. Cohen, Plato's *The Republic*, translated by D. P. Lee, Virgil's *The Pastoral Poems*, translated by E. V. Rieu; Princeton University Press for *Old English Poetry*, by J. D. Spaeth; Routledge & Kegan Paul for *Tractatus Logico-Philosophicus*, by L. Wittgenstein; University of California Press for *The Literary Riddle before 1600* and *English Riddles from Oral Tradition*, by A. Taylor, *Clareti Enigmata*, edited by F. Peachy; University of Minnesota Press for *The Book of Apollonius*, translated by R. L. Grismer and E. Atkins; A. P. Watt and the Executors of the Estate of C. L. Dodgson for part of a letter from Lewis Carroll to his sister.